A JOHN CATT PUBLICATION

Sonia Thompson

BERGER'S
AN ETHIC OF EXCELLENCE
IN ACTION

IN ACTION | EDITOR
SERIES | **TOM SHERRINGTON**

COVER ILLUSTRATION BY
OLIVER CAVIGLIOLI | A **WALKTHRUs** PRODUCTION

First Published 2022

by John Catt Educational Ltd,
15 Riduna Park, Station Road,
Melton, Woodbridge IP12 1QT

Tel: +44 (0) 1394 389850
Email: enquiries@johncatt.com
Website: www.johncatt.com

© **2022 Sonia Thompson**
Illustrations by Oliver Caviglioli

ISBN: 978 1 913622 99 2

Set and designed by John Catt Educational Limited

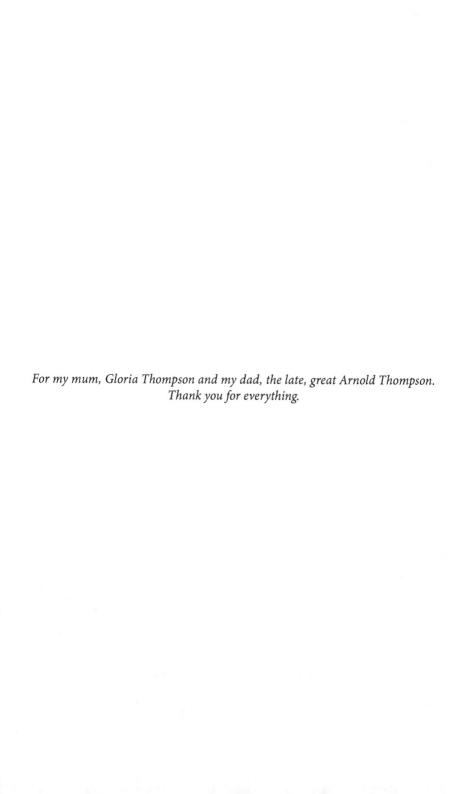

For my mum, Gloria Thompson and my dad, the late, great Arnold Thompson.
Thank you for everything.

TOM SHERRINGTON

The idea for the *In Action* series was developed by John Catt's *Teaching WalkThrus* team after we saw how popular our *Rosenshine's Principles in Action* booklets proved to be. We realised that the same approach might support teachers to access the ideas of a range of researchers, cognitive scientists and educators. A constant challenge that we wrestle with in the world of teaching and education research is the significant distance between the formulation of a set of concepts and conclusions that might be useful to teachers and the moment when a teacher uses those ideas to teach their students in a more effective manner, thereby succeeding in securing deeper or richer learning. Sometimes so much meaning is lost along that journey, through all the communication barriers that line the road, that the implementation of the idea bears no relation to the concept its originator had in mind. Sometimes it's more powerful to hear from a teacher about how they implemented an idea than it is to read about the idea from a researcher or cognitive scientist directly – because they reduce that distance; they push some of those barriers aside.

In our *In Action* series, the authors and their collaborative partners are all teachers or school leaders close to the action in classrooms in real schools. Their strategies for translating their subjects' work into practice bring fresh energy to a powerful set of original ideas in a way that we're confident will support teachers with their professional learning and, ultimately, their classroom practice. In doing so, they are also paying their respects to the original researchers and their work. In education, as in so many walks of life, we are standing on the shoulders of giants. We believe that our selection of featured researchers and papers represents some of the most important work done in the field of education in recent times.

This *In Action* book is rather different to some of the others in the series in that it begins with ideas rooted in practice rather than in research studies. Ron Berger is widely recognised by thousands of teachers as the man who gave us Austin's Butterfly – the classic educational story told in a video used in countless training sessions at all levels. However, as we learn in this book, Austin's story – and the multi-layered message it conveys – is just one of many elements of Berger's wonderful book *An Ethic of Excellence*, which reports on the findings of a long career in teaching and school leadership. It's been an extremely influential book, regularly cited by educators among their favourite references, and it was an early decision to try to include it in the *In Action* series. I first met Sonia Thompson at a training event where she kept the audience enthralled with the story of the achievements and philosophy of her wonderful school St Matthew's in Birmingham. I was completely inspired by how Sonia combined fiercely high expectations with an earnest engagement with cognitive science and research in general and a commitment to reading and developing children's empathy. She shared the profound idea that all children arrive to school with their 'backpacks' of life experience and culture that make them who they are and that schools must allow children that knowledge to be shared and celebrated.

When we discussed *Berger In Action*, Sonia was immediately thrilled to have a chance to share her love for *An Ethic of Excellence*, so much of which resonates with practice in her school. Similarly, Ron was delighted when Sonia approached him and he has provided significant encouragement during the writing process. It's a real honour that he agreed to write the foreword which emphasises the value of beautiful work. Sonia was determined to include photographs of the exemplars she refers to and I'm grateful to all her contributors and the editorial team at John Catt for making that possible.

FOREWORD

RON BERGER

Last week I was out to dinner with my wife and friends when our conversation was interrupted. A woman tentatively approached us with the welcome face of someone I had not seen in over 35 years. 'Mr. B?' she asked. I smiled at her: 'Juliet, you look wonderful.' She was taken aback. 'How did you recognise me? I haven't seen you since sixth grade.' Then her sisters Jessica and Mariah appeared beside her, and her brother Caleb – all former students of mine from the 1980s, together for the holidays. We hugged, despite pandemic cautions, and they proudly caught me up on their lives, their careers, their children, and graciously gave me a copy of Caleb's striking new book of photography. There is no greater gift as a teacher than to see former students doing well and to have been some part of that success.

Another gift of my life as an educator is that my book *An Ethic of Excellence: Building a Culture of Craftsmanship in Students* continues to be printed and used by teachers around the world after almost 20 years, and that teachers still find it an affirmation of why they are proud of their work. I have been working in education for more than 45 years, and though I continue to learn more every day, my core message has not changed at all. I am privileged to work with schools and districts around the world and share with them this simple truth: in life we are not measured by test scores, but rather by two things – the quality of who we are as human beings, and the quality of the work we do. School is a place to cultivate character in children and to produce beautiful work – to contribute to a better world.

I am honoured to be included in Tom Sherrington's terrific *In Action* series in this powerful book by Sonia Thompson. Sonia is an inspirational school leader committed to this vision of excellence and she understands deeply that the core work does not lie in the specific practices of models, critique, and feedback – as valuable as they are. Our core work is to build school cultures that promote excellence all day long. In Sonia's words, describing her school, St. Matthews, '... this is what our school culture is built upon: the dogged determination to help our students achieve beyond what they think is possible.'

She recognises that this begins with the ethic and mindset of her staff and says, 'It is not strange for us to talk about being "our very best selves".' It includes her broader community, using an asset-based lens for the school's families to 'challenge and disrupt taken for granted assumptions and perceptions of families such as ours'. And she understands that this work for excellence for every student is at the heart of work for educational equity: 'Establishing an *equitable culture* (italics mine) acts as the cornerstone for what we feel are our high expectations for teaching, learning, behaviour and learning behaviours.'

When we speak about *beautiful work*, we need to lift up this work of Sonia and her staff, and of all of you as educators and your teammates, right alongside Austin's Butterfly.

ACKNOWLEDGEMENTS

The first thank you must go to Ron Berger, the wonderful author of *An Ethic of Excellence*. In chapter 3, he has read each section and offered feedback in the most supportive of ways. I thank him for his kindness and continue to be amazed at his humility. In an email to me he wrote, 'It's gratifying to see your thoughtfulness in the explication of these ideas. I am always so appreciative to see that the idea of kind, specific and helpful peer feedback has been used well by so many different educators around the world.'

I owe nothing but gratitude and praise to my Senior Leadership Team and brilliant section writers, Tracey Adams (deputy headteacher), Hydeh Fayaz (lead practitioner/Year 1 teacher) and Daniel Martin, who was my assistant headteacher and is now a deputy head at another school. They were focused and driven to not only research and write but to do it all while teaching, in the most challenging of COVID-19 times. I hope they are all as excited as I am about the book.

Thank you to all the educators who sent in case studies. I really appreciate your time and amazing effort.

Mark Gregory, thank you for recommending me for Leverage Leadership training and being such a supporter and thank you to my Leverage Leadership Institute tutors, Paul Bambrick-Santoyo, Kathleen Sullivan, Riyad Mohammed and Cohort 8. This professional development has been some of the best I have ever attended, both intellectually and emotionally. It has heavily influenced my thinking and this book.

Finally, I would like to thank and totally appreciate Tom Sherrington. We first met at a training day, in Portishead, where we were both delivering – Tom in the morning (of course his session was inspiring) and me in the afternoon. I thought he would leave after but to my surprise he stayed and to say I was nervous was an understatement. We made friends that day. When I received the email from Tom, asking me if I would like to be part of the *In Action* family, I was shocked, surprised and honoured. Throughout this process, he has been patient, kind, encouraging and doubly patient and for that I am absolutely grateful.

TABLE OF CONTENTS

INTRODUCTION

SONIA THOMPSON

Source: Sherrington and Caviglioli (2020) Teaching WalkThrus: Five-step guides to instructional coaching.

'If you're going to do something, I believe you should do it well. You should sweat over it and make sure it is strong and accurate and beautiful and you should be proud of it.'

Ron Berger

To begin with, I want to define the two key words in the title of this book:

- Ethic – an idea or moral belief that influences the behaviour, attitudes, and philosophy of a group of people.
- Excellence – the state or quality of excelling or being exceptionally good; extreme merit; superiority (Collins Cobuild online dictionary, 2021).

I have summarised this as **a moral imperative to strive towards greatness.**

This *In Action* book exists because Ron Berger's *An Ethic of Excellence* is a seminal read. A bold claim, but one I fully stand by. It is one of the soundtracks to an educational journey that I am indubitably still on, and it continues to covertly and overtly walk me through many teacher/leader and headteacher awakenings. The most impactful and pronounced of these is the criticality of embedding excellence into schools' everyday practices, not as an incidental or an accident, but as an actual ethic.

Berger is clear that for any school striving for excellence every day, the process is never fast. Rather, it is slow and deliberate and takes patience and time. If this investment is made, the centrality of excellence as an ethic in altering the trajectory of what can be achieved, by both students and teachers, is unrivalled. On my initial readings of Berger's book, it was this certainty of return that caught my attention. I was determined to transubstantiate the ethics into my teaching, leading and finally, into my headship armoury.

I am not alone in discerning the payoffs. There is a raft of teachers, leaders and schools, in the UK and around the world, who hold this book in high esteem. To name a few, John Tomsett, Mary Myatt, Alex Quigley and Tom Sherrington have all either drawn on or endorsed Berger's thinking. For Allison and Tharby (2015), when introducing their brilliant book, they call the value of excellence 'the bedrock for everything that follows'. They go on to write that, 'we realised that in our headlong pursuit of fashionable pedagogical ideas – such as pace, rapid progress and independent learning – we had long neglected an eternal truth. That it is our fundamental responsibility to give children the chance to be excellent.' This is a testament to the leverage of this small but mighty masterpiece and its author.

Always striving for excellence

As a newly qualified teacher in the mid-1980s, excellence, as I now understand it, was a thought and a belief that propelled me to do more, read more and ultimately want and demand more from my students. I am not ashamed to say that I really did not know what I was doing half of the time, but what I knew to be true was that if I did not begin to strengthen my subject knowledge and believe that my students could achieve more, my students would not move forward. So, I began to put in the work. I knew I was getting it wrong and I learned to accept that this was part of the process. That in itself was not easy but I was definitely up for the challenge. Mary Myatt (2016) states, 'We are a challenge-seeking species. The leaders who understand this are prepared, first of all, to push themselves.' It was this dogged and often confused determination that ultimately began to bear fruit. Students began to make progress and leaders began to notice what I was doing in my classroom and positively comment on it. I began to feel pride, as a teacher, and I wanted this feeling to stick. To sustain this, I quickly understood that I needed to keep doing what I was doing; begin to unpick what I was doing, codify it (while still thinking flexibly), and strive to do it even better.

An Ethic of Excellence – a manual for lasting change

The difficulty with this was that although the 'edu-writing' world was present, it was not as accessible, or dare I say vibrant, to teachers as it is now. So, my first reading (of many) of *An Ethic of Excellence* was, as I said, fundamental and profound.

Berger, a coalface teacher and master carpenter, was telling us teachers that we were in a scholarly profession. He encouraged us to take responsibility to not only hone our craft for ourselves but also to be 'determined to find success' for our students. I look back now on that first reading (as the headteacher of a school in an area of high disadvantage), and realise that what I gained from that reading was an undeniable strength that I could do more to affect change in my students. Berger had as much respect and ambition for his students and for teachers as I did.

What was even more extraordinary, was that without any form of research base, Berger attempted to codify the strategies, the toolboxes and what they could look like. Paul Bambrick-Santoyo (2018) calls these 'replicable results'. He went on to say, when writing about schools that were succeeding for their students, despite the odds, 'these leaders didn't succeed in some idiosyncratic way: they used replicable systems and structures, that others can follow. The successes these leaders built were not the product of unique charisma; they came from strategies that any leader can apply.'

In this same vein, what Berger presented to me and other readers, were repeatable, teachable strategies that can be applied from class teacher to school leader. It was nothing less than a revelation and an absolute revolution.

Ron Berger – Teacher par excellence

The power of *An Ethic of Excellence* is embedded within the context of its author and hero of the book Ron Berger. His anecdotes chronicling his experiences, deeply held beliefs and passions for what teachers and schools can achieve, are all consuming and awe-inspiring. The fact that he is a teacher 'leading a double life' as a master carpenter is even more extraordinary and wonderful.

Berger uses his master carpentry to not only analogise his educational practices but to punctuate and clarify his messages around:

1. Being proud, and
2. Finding beauty in both what we, as educators/scholars, do and what our children do/have the potential to achieve.

Cuthbert and Standish (2021) are clear when they distinguish this thinking and propose 'that a school curriculum should challenge pupils to consider moral (what is right), aesthetic (what is beauty) and epistemological (what is true) questions'.

This clarity permeates when you read Berger's definition of a craftsman: 'Someone who has integrity and knowledge, who is dedicated to his work and who is proud of what he does and who he is. Someone who thinks carefully and does things well.'

In the book, this is what Berger wants the reader to align with. As an educator and scholar, reading this was an 'aha' moment. In *An Ethic of Excellence*, there are so many 'aha' moments and that is what has drawn and continues to draw so many to it.

'If it ain't broke, don't fix it' – why link research to *An Ethic of Excellence?*

Up to this point, the *In Action* series has featured books that are underpinned by an evidence base or theory. These have often been linked to a particular cognitive scientist and/or researcher. *An Ethic of Excellence* does not have any of that. There is no evidence base from controlled trials; no theories or models that link to any researchers or psychologists. It is solely Berger's own 'theories', musings and stories. As he writes, 'I bring no blueprint for school change … there are many models of excellence. The tools I offer are strategies, models and metaphors and along with them, I have classroom stories…'

For me, reading *An Ethic of Excellence* again, this time as a headteacher interested in evidence-informed practice and the Director of an Education Endowment Foundation (EEF) Research School, it was the 'aha' moments all over again. Only this time, my brain was making various connections to books, theories, researchers, blogs and professional development and it was this relatedness that led to this guise of the book, *Berger's An Ethic of Excellence in Action.*

How to read this book

In the book, we will attempt to analyse some of the toolbox strategies; the ones that resonated the most with us and that we felt could be applied across all ages and phases. As stated, we placed our thinking within a framework of relevant research and then aimed to corroborate Berger's strategies/ethics, as they apply to classroom practice.

We have attempted to align all of our thinking around and be mindful of Berger's key principles:

- Assign work that matters.
- Study examples of excellence.
- Build a culture of critique.
- Require multiple revisions.
- Provide opportunities for public presentation.

This book follows the same format as Berger's, in that it also has the three toolboxes – which he states are the 'strategies, models and metaphors'. Berger writes metaphorically 'to make the strategies more easily referenced for the reader'.

These toolboxes can be summarised as:

- **The first toolbox: A School Culture of Excellence** – creating/embedding a community that encourages and supports excellence.
- **The second toolbox: Work of Excellence** – improving the quality of student work and thinking. Berger calls this 'the big heavy one ... the heart of my work with schools'.
- **The third toolbox: Teaching of Excellence** – teachers improving through bringing passion and scholarship to the role.

This book then fixes a lens on a few key areas. In chapter 2, the first toolbox, we unpick culture and community. Like Berger, we 'heavy-lift' in the second toolbox and delve deeper into four strategies in sections 1 to 4 of chapter 3. Finally, in chapter 4, the third toolbox, we look at supporting teachers and scholarship.

Active ingredients

Each chapter and section ends with a summary of Berger's strategy for improving students' work and thinking. These points serve to support practitioners to understand what they might want to do in order to move this strategy forward. They are by no means definitive or fixed. As I was writing this book and rereading *An Ethic of Excellence*, this brought to mind the ideas of 'active ingredients'.

Jonathan Haslam (2020) writes in his blog, 'If we know what the "active ingredients" are of, let's say, feedback, we know the bits that must be included for it to have an impact, and the bits that we can tweak for local conditions.' These key points are for you to know what to include when implementing the strategy and what to adapt for your context.

As you read this book, please do not feel that my school, St Matthew's, is putting itself on an excellence pedestal. As all schools, we are on a journey and fully recognise that achieving excellence is a never-ending marathon, not a sprint.

We hope you enjoy either revisiting, refreshing or renewing your appreciation of Berger's strategies, models and metaphors, alongside the research and practice. If *An Ethic of Excellence* is new to you, I hope this book will give you an insight into how Berger's concept of excellence can be effectively discussed and potentially implemented with your own context.

References.

Allison, S. and Tharby, A. (2015) *Making every lesson count.* Wales: Crown House Publishing.

Bambrick-Santoyo, P. (2018) *Leverage Leadership 2.0: A practical guide to building exceptional schools.* San Francisco, USA: Jossey-Bass.

Collins Cobuild Online Dictionary. (2021) Available at: www.collinsdictionary.com (Accessed: 10 December 2021).

Cuthbert, A. and Standish, A. (eds.) (2021) *What should schools teach? Disciplines, subjects and the pursuit of truth.* 2nd ed. London: UCL Press, p. 9.

Fletcher-Wood, H. (2013) *How can we create 'An Ethic of Excellence' in our schools?* Available at: https://improvingteaching.co.uk/2013/11/10/how-can-we-create-an-ethic-of-excellence-in-our-schools/ (Accessed: 21 December 2021).

Haslam, J. (2020) *What are active ingredients?* The Institute for Effective Education. Available at: https://the-iee.org.uk/2020/10/22/what-are-active-ingredients/ (Accessed: 10 December 2021).

Myatt, M. (2016) *High challenge, low threat: Finding the balance.* Woodbridge: John Catt Educational Ltd, p. 11.

Tomsett, J. (2015) *This much I know about love over fear.* Wales: Crown House Publishing.

Quigley, A. (2012) *A taste of Berger: Reading 'An Ethic of Excellence'.* Available at: www.theconfidentteacher.com/2012/10/a-taste-of-berger-reading-an-ethic-of-excellence/ (Accessed: 21 December 2021).

CHAPTER 1

THE PRESENTATION OF AUSTIN'S BUTTERFLY

SONIA THOMPSON

'The progress of the drawing, from a primitive first draft to an impressive final is a powerful message for educators ... we often settle for low-quality work because we underestimate the capacity of students to create great work. With time, clarity, critique and support, students are capable of much more than we imagine.'

Ron Berger

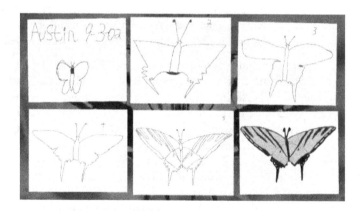

You may not have read *An Ethic of Excellence* but if you are a teacher and do not know Austin's Butterfly, then you have either been living and teaching in a cave, or have never attended an INSET day, in the whole of the UK, over the past few years. Equally, you may just not know Austin or his butterfly. If you do not, I would implore you to watch the video. I am absolutely confident enough in its content to say that it will transform your thinking about feedback.

Austin's Butterfly – YouTube

Austin's Butterfly is the exemplification of the veracity of the 'paradigm shift' that Berger calls for in the second toolbox's examination of critique. In fact, as Berger himself stated when he was giving me feedback on the chapter, 'The one push that I would give to you, is to elevate the Austin's Butterfly multiple-draft process as foundational – which it is, to my thinking.' The six-minute video of a group of first-grade children provides the viewer with a model of teaching that is so powerful. Berger not only illustrates, he also illuminates the strength of focused critique and how it can very quickly change what was a mundane drawing into a well-crafted and thoughtful replication of the original butterfly photograph. Again, as Berger stated in feedback to me, 'Once we decide it requires a final draft, *then* it is essential that it goes through an iterative process, with critique from peers (and sometimes, hopefully, from outside experts from the community or professional world), and has an audience beyond the teacher.'

The specificity of the 'kind, helpful and specific' feedback is deliberately cultivated by Berger, and it is heart-warming to see the children 'kindly but specifically' suggest what Austin needs to do. What stood out to me the most, was the artful questioning of the children by Berger that enabled the feedback to have the impact on the drawer that it had. I would argue that the impact on those giving feedback would have been just as powerful and it is this convergent opportunity that teachers need to harness, through the use of drafts. Allison and Tharby (2015) write, 'Keep copies of each draft of the work of students who have made particularly impressive progress. Use these to model the journey to success – from the flawed first draft to the beautiful final piece.' There will be more on this in chapter 3.

Ultimately though, it is the movement of the drawing from basic to its glorious scientific finality that is the essence of the video, for all practitioners. It is an essence that challenges all the low expectations and low-quality work we often accept and the realisation that if we underestimate the capacity of students, we sell them short. *Teaching WalkThrus* by Sherrington and Caviglioli (2020) quotes the great Bill Rogers, 'You establish what you establish … if in practice you tolerate mediocre work … you have established that this is the norm so this is what you will get.' For with time, tenacity and techniques, they are actually capable of achieving greater than we can imagine. Like Berger, I think we owe this to all of our students, particularly those in areas of high disadvantage, to support our students to critique and revise to the highest standard. As Hammond (2015) states, 'Our students belong in academic spaces and it is our job to create the environment that welcomes them, so that they are able to intellectually flourish.'

Active ingredients: Austin's Butterfly is...

- A great model of critique and revision for students and teachers of all ages; it has been used as a metaphor for improvement by students from kindergarten to high school, and by teachers and school leaders. It is a clear, visual image of the reason to have high standards and systems for improving work.

- Specific changes in his drawings being linked to very specific feedback from peers, illuminating the need for critique to be targeted and specific.

- An inspirational model of the power of perseverance and revision to improve quality.

- An example of how we often stop short in school from pushing students to a high level of quality.

References.

Allison, S. and Tharby, A. (2015) *Making every lesson count*. Wales: Crown House Publishing, p. 102.

Hammond, Z. (2015) *Culturally responsive teaching and the brain: Promoting authentic engagement and rigor among culturally and linguistically diverse students*. USA: Corwin, Sage.

Sherrington, T. and Caviglioli, O. (2020) *Teaching WalkThrus: Five-step guides to instructional coaching*. Woodbridge: John Catt Educational Ltd, p. 38.

CHAPTER 2

THE FIRST TOOLBOX: A SCHOOL CULTURE OF EXCELLENCE

SONIA THOMPSON

'The key to excellence is this: it is born from culture. When children enter a family culture, a community culture, or a school culture that demands and supports excellence, they work to fit into that culture. A culture of excellence transcends race, class, and geography … Once those children enter a culture with a powerful ethic, that ethic becomes their norm. It's what they know.'

Ron Berger

It is not surprising that the cornerstone of *An Ethic of Excellence* is culture. Coates (2017) states that, 'Whenever we engage with human groupings we encounter culture. These are behaviours, attitudes, values and procedures that serve to delineate a particular group. Sometimes these are overt, declared and enforced, as for example, in a military context. In many organisations they are multi-layered and amorphous.' Within education, culture is vociferously discussed and written about in many educational texts. Theorists generally accept that it is crucial for any school to function and thrive. What is also concrete and probably more contextual are the variables around what can make a school culture successful.

For Berger, culture matters to the extent that without it, strategies and ethics will not be valuable, sustainable or engrained within the fabric of any setting. From an ethic perspective, it governs student achievement, and it is this reciprocal relationship that means that where it is not engrained, students' attitudes and efforts will adjust/lessen to fit that perspective. Watson (2001) writes, 'If the culture is not hospitable to learning then student achievement can suffer.'

Berger details how family culture, neighbourhood culture and school culture all contribute to what a student can potentially achieve. Students will adapt their behaviours based on what these cultures dictate. Berger challenges schools when he states, 'Schools need to consciously shape their cultures to be spaces where it's safe to care, where it's cool to care. They need to reach out to family and neighbourhood cultures to support this.'

Why culture matters at St Matthew's

Like all schools, we would like to think we have **culture with a powerful ethic**. There is a deliberate clarity in St Matthew's vision, values and mission statement. I feel that a lot of this is bound to being a church school but over the years, as we have lived and breathed our culture and ethos, it has cemented the 'why' and given us a newfound determination to embed our school principles, for the sake of our children and our community.

The 'St Matthew's Way', or as Bennett (2017) states, 'the way we do things round here', is a phrase that is often used about our school. It epitomises the high expectations, challenge and ambition we have for our children and for each other. I am proud when visitors say that they can feel 'it' as soon as they walk through the door and are greeted by a child with a 'Hello', a 'Good morning' or a 'Welcome to St Matthew's, can I help you?'

Our culture is unique to our context because we (our school community) have shaped it by deciding what we wanted for our school. So, if we wanted our children to greet visitors, we had to teach them to do that. If we wanted exceptional behaviour, we had to model that and demand and expect it every day.

A couple of weeks into the school year, the classes hold a parent meeting. This is where we set out our stall. This is where we are able to communicate our culture to parents and share our vision of high expectations, challenge and ambition for their children. We also communicate the part we want/expect parents to play. As a school that values the capital that our children bring to school, we encourage a sense of reciprocity and ownership of our cultural school norms. It's not about taking away from what they do, but to add the disciplinary (what they can only learn from teachers) elements to it. Parents are invited to Celebration Assemblies every Friday. They are able to see how we value quality, beauty – as defined in *An Ethic of Excellence* – behaviour and kindness, and that these are our social norms.

The ethos that underpins our 'why?'

Our mottos, vision and values set the standard for our excellence. As Mary Myatt states, 'We know what we are offering to our children and the reason why.'

Mottos:

'With God, nothing is impossible' and 'You are the light of the world.'

Mission statement:

'St Matthew's is a community of learners; planning, pursuing and providing excellence and enjoyment through Christian values. Children are valued for their individuality and heritage. They are supported and motivated to fulfil their potential, in order to meet the challenges of a changing society.'

When we composed the mission statement, all of our school community was involved. Our brief was to succinctly capture our ambition for our children and for each other. We wanted it to have longevity and to be able to hold us accountable; to always do our utmost for our children, in order for them to succeed, within a culture of excellence.

Values – CAP:

C – Courage: Team St Matthew's does not give up. We look back in history to prepare ourselves for the future.

A – Attainment: Team St Matthew's focuses on results and we do whatever it takes to achieve our goals. We push ourselves beyond what we think is possible.

P – Pride: Team St Matthew's values excellence in all that we do. We think and act as our own best selves.

'Wear your CAP with dignity' or 'Gere pileum cum dignate' (because we teach Latin).

We have enabled our children to live this ethos through the high expectations around behaviour and building their attitudes to learning. Our children want to learn and they love to learn. That is what they tell us. Their eagerness to learn more challenging stuff is infectious and drives our determination to do whatever we can to realise this.

Over the years, as this ethos has embedded, it has allowed our teachers the uninterrupted space to work and drive forward excellence... and it needs to be deliberately driven, as it does not just happen. Allison and Tharby (2015) comment, 'But excellence is hard to come by. To achieve it, a child must work hard and be prepared to face the setbacks they will inevitably meet on the journey.' So, we talk about our excellence every day through our daily assemblies, but we have always had to be mindful. Fritzgerald (2020) stated in her framework, 'Sometimes we tout mission statements, vision statements, and goals that include buzzwords that everyone says and everyone can recite but only a few actually live the words out. You can tell what is most important by who is achieving the most.' For Coates (2017), 'not only is generating the appropriate culture a high priority for leaders but that the concept has a synergy with mission, vision and value statements. If the three statements are afforded a centrality and engaged with consistently then they become powerful tools to explore and shape culture.' Because of this, we shaped our most current review on these; our golden threads – excellence and equity.

An equitable culture

Establishing an equitable culture acts as the cornerstone for what we feel are our high expectations of excellence for teaching, learning, behaviour and learning behaviours. Equity and culture, for this purpose, are defined by the National Equity Project as:

Equity	Culture
Equity can be defined as anything that is aimed at: 1. Ensuring equally high outcomes for all participants in our educational system; **removing the predictability of success or failures that currently correlates with any social or cultural factor;** 2. Interrupting inequitable practices, examining biases, and creating inclusive multicultural school environments for adults and children; and 3. Discovering and cultivating the unique gifts, talents and interests that every human possesses.	A pattern of values, benefits and expectations shared by a group's members that powerfully shapes the behaviours of individuals within the group.

From this, we took the statements that pushed our recent thinking forward, 'removing the predictability of success or failures that currently correlates with any social or cultural factor' and 'interrupting inequitable practices...' This now functions alongside our mission, as an EEF Research School: 'The Education Endowment Foundation (EEF) is dedicated to breaking the link between family income and educational achievement.' Having shared and discussed them with teachers, they both definitely provide a powerful backdrop for our whole school's next steps.

Having restated our 'why', we then re-examined our 'how'. We did this as part of our implementation of Leverage Leadership (I am a 2021-22 fellow of Leverage Leadership Institute and it is impacting on all areas of St Matthew's... and this book), both inside and outside of the classroom. All routines and procedures – including preparing for lunchtime (which we identified as a problem) – needed a reset.

Excellence and equity linked perfectly to a quote from a Leverage Leadership training course I attended in 2021: 'Values inform expectations. Expectations influence behaviour. Behaviour creates culture.' Therefore, the reset began with this.

Resetting our routines and procedures for excellence

'Productive, positive and powerful learning environments are promoted by predictable routines.' (This was also quoted at the Leverage Leadership course.) As a school, we set out how to codify this, being mindful that we all needed to understand what we were committing to.

What would this look/sound like? What message were we sending to the students?

- Interactions with parents and visitors at the school office.
- How (and why) our site manager maintains the school building.

For Berger, 'A clean and well-kept building guarantees nothing about the quality of work children will accomplish within it. But it matters. It's a message. It's a visual model of the ethic within the building. The building doesn't have to be a palace ... but it has to show the children, the teachers and the parents that somebody cares about them.'

At St Matthew's, the clear message to all, once understood as an ethic, has led to all striving to embed it.

- Governors' expectations for the HT/leaders.
- Assemblies/collective worship. The opportunity to bring our children together for assemblies daily acts as a focal point for excellence – expectations of high ambition, quality, resilience and an expectation that these things are our norm, part of our culture and are 'what we do', all the time. In fact, we use this opportunity to reinforce that anything less is not good enough. It is not strange for us to talk about being 'our very best selves' – using our values statements to remind our children that 'nothing is impossible' and that they are the 'lights of the world'. This

is also communicated in expectations about uniform, punctuality and attendance, our manners, respect and empathy for others.

- PSHE and wellbeing.
- All subject areas.
- Interactions with children at playtimes, lunchtimes, mornings and end of day.

For this, we went back to Bambrick-Santoyo's *Leverage Leadership* (2018) and plotted what we wanted excellence to look like for all involved.

End of day dismissal

Productive, positive, and powerful learning environments are promoted by predictable routines

Timings	Teacher	Teaching Assistant	Children
2.40pm – Finish final lesson for the day	• Giving clear instructions to pupils/monitors for tidying up: classroom, pencil pots/pencil cases, resources and books • Monitor and scan room	• Monitor and scan room to support tidying up process • Support children who need particular support with this routine	• Tidying up • Sit down and show they are ready once this is done
2.50pm – End-of-day read aloud begins for 20 minutes	• Reading class novel or texts with intonation • Engaging with children, while reading	• Tidy up all classroom areas • Re-sharpen pencils • Complete additional jobs assigned by the teacher	• Relax and listen attentively to the story • Engage and participate when needed
3.10pm – End of day prayer/ Collect belongings *If on PPA, teacher should be back in the classroom.* *NB to go to the hall, to set up for clubs.*	• Lead routine of: – Reciting school prayer – hands together and eyes closed – as we finish – Stack chairs – Dismiss groups to collect belongings and line up	• Monitor and scan cloakroom and line to support process • Ensure children have coats and all belongs go into a bag	• Prayer – All children to participate • Collect belongings – Put belongings into bag – Put on coat
3.15pm – Bell rings/leave school	• Teacher to lead children out (with a copy of passwords) and ensure no running or dawdling • Teacher to look back, and monitor and scan line • Final greeting as children go – have a good evening, specific messages	• Stay at back of line to monitor and scan	• Walk in a line

This consistency and predictability of messages from all involved within our school community has been and still is key to our success. This is not just about attainment data but it is the A in CAP. As a school in Nechells, one of the most deprived areas in Birmingham and Britain, school leaders are fully aware that there are many distractions, challenges, family issues and preconceived/negative ideas from other adults about children from this area. Our role in ensuring that all of our school community has high expectations and that we will accept no excuses for poor standards of conduct is crucial. The message is, we are committed to seeing our children flourish.

A curriculum for excellence – celebrating diversity, enabling flourishing

The term 'flourish' holds a lot of weight within our Church of England school setting. For me, it is a call to an excellence ethic. Ford and Wolfe in *Called, Connected, Committed* state, 'Leaders in education cherish diversity and inclusion, recognising that their communities are inherently better and richer in their differences. They take every opportunity to celebrate learning together, and hold their doors open to people from all backgrounds and traditions. Leaders unlock opportunities for their children to flourish in a wide variety of disciplines, not simply those that are measured.'

In my chapter in *The researchED Guide to The Curriculum* (2020), I outline how we have worked hard to ensure that our curriculum, our values and our mission statement converge and communicate to our children and teachers that we are 'unflinching' about the business of education. When we composed the mission statement, all of our school community was involved. But in all of this, I am mindful of not ever wanting to portray our children as deficit. This is particularly pertinent because the majority of our children are from black and minority ethnic backgrounds, as are many of my teachers. We are strident about the need for there to be a co-existence between, and a deference to, the rich cultural capital that our children and our teachers bring into our school; and the rich capital and traditions of this country.

In his section on supporting a community inside and out, Berger comments on how for this to be lived out, 'children are given a chance to share from their home life'. For us, the evidence-based work of Gonzalez et al. (2005) has supported us to proudly expose the space within our curriculum to not only acknowledge heritage and culture but to place its deep richness at the heart of our curriculum. Gonzalez calls this '**funds of knowledge**' and states that these are the 'rich repositories of accumulated knowledge found present in households and communities'.

At St Matthew's, we wanted to 'challenge and disrupt taken for granted assumptions and perceptions about families' such as ours. Instead, we seek to find out about 'personal passions, ways of learning outside school, popular cultural interests and their everyday literacy practices and experiences.' So, at the beginning of each of our subject weeks, children, families and teachers 'share their literacy lives' and benefit greatly from learning about each other and what makes us the 'diverse humans' that we are. Our whole-school themes called 'The Six Ours' enable this to happen. We begin the year with 'Our Lives, Our Family', we go on to, 'Our Community', 'Our World', 'Our Passions', 'Our Global Village' and finally, 'Our Future'.

Gonzalez writes that, 'understanding the funds of knowledge within a community and a family is important for a teacher. He/she can tap into this knowledge and use it to help acquire new knowledge.' So, at St Matthew's through the 'Ours', we are able to share stories about our families and culture, including where our families are from and why they came to England. I have shared with the children information about my heritage and the things that I value and make my culture so rich. Teachers and children have shared pictures of siblings and themselves and our parents have shared stories from their cultures and invited us to share their journeys and how this has influenced their current lifestyles.

We also have an open-door policy, as well as having a dedicated 'Parents to School Day', as part of our subject weeks. Parents can directly input into all foundation subject teaching. Cremin et al. (2004) state, 'Many schools view parents primarily as supporters of schoolwork, rather than seeing them as a source of different and/or complementary literacy and learning experiences.' It is this reciprocity that has strengthened our school community and like Berger's experience, we are all the better for it.

This vision for excellence, for our children and for ourselves as educators has brought us so far but we cannot and will not be complacent. Like curriculum, our culture, equity and excellence must be responsive to our context and our community. For us, this is why being evidence-informed matters.

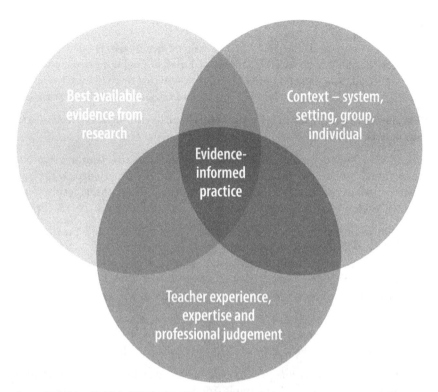

Source: Stefanini and Griffiths (2020) Addressing the challenges of using evidence in education.

We are determined to build on the richness that is already there and take it deeper and wider, so that our children, from Nechells, Birmingham, can soar to heights that not even we (with our vision for excellence) think is possible.

Case study

Janine Ashman and Catrina Battista are co-headteachers at Unlocking Excellence English Hub based at St Peter's Church of England Primary School, in Portishead. It is one of 34 English Hubs designated by the Department for Education. Janine tweets @JanineAshman and Catrina @catrin_battista.

'Excellence in excellence in all we do, excellence in who we are, excellence in our service with others.'

We are proud to offer children at St Peter's an innovative, exciting and rigorous curriculum. As well as thinking carefully about the knowledge, skills and qualities that we want children to learn and develop, we also think deeply about *how* we teach this curriculum to ensure that every child can achieve excellence.

Through examination of world-class educational research and practice, we have developed our own unique pedagogy. *An Ethic of Excellence* was one of those practices. We call this 'Excellence as Standard' and it forms the central core to all our teaching and learning across the school. It underpins how every learner in our community will learn, including staff as well as children.

Our school vision (excellence in all we do, excellence in who we are, excellence in our service with others) and Excellence as Standard pedagogy are embedded into everything we do at St Peter's – for both adults and children.

As a large school, our vision gives us a common pedagogical framework, which is central to all of our teaching and learning practices. The focus on enacting our vision has given us the confidence to know that across our 21 classes, all children are receiving the same expert teaching. This gives our children a strong foundation of key knowledge and skills, which supports them to deepen their learning.

To embed our Culture of Excellence, we have ensured that:

- Staff professional development supports and deepens understanding and links to relevant research within each of our key areas of teaching and learning.

- We explicitly teach children about our pedagogy so they understand why we teach in this way and how they can develop these skills in their learning.

- At the beginning of each academic year we induct children into our pedagogy through our 'Excellence Exhibition'. This is a two-week programme where we unpick what our 'Excellence as Standard' culture means at St Peter's. This includes watching Austin's Butterfly. Alongside this, every class works on producing an expert piece of artwork, in order to apply the skills and dispositions we are developing. This results in an art exhibition across the whole school, with around a thousand visitors and members of the school community.

- All of our teaching will use and explicitly refer to aspects of our Excellence as Standard pedagogy.

Using these principles has enabled us to develop a strong pedagogy that supports teachers to ensure our pupils move from novices to experts in their learning.

Excellence as Standard

Through examination of world-class educational research and practice we have **developed** our own unique pedagogy – or way of teaching.
We call this *'Excellence as Standard'* and it forms the central core to all our teaching and learning across the whole school.

Our pedagogy – **Excellence as Standard**
– has 5 distinct strands which are embedded into teaching at St Peter's.

Purpose

We believe that children learn best when they have an authentic purpose for their learning.

- We give children a real audience for their work whenever possible.
- We reach out beyond school to local and national organisations to provide meaningful contexts for learning.
- Each year, every child is given the opportunity to serve and improve their local community through *'Legacy Learning projects'*.

Critique

To develop and grow, we need a culture of growth mindset where we all believe we can develop and improve. This means we need to receive and give feedback and critique – recognising strengths but also knowing how to improve.

- We have a culture and common language of critique that is kind, helpful and specific.
- We explicitly teach children how to give critique and also act on it when they are the receiver.
- We have high expectations of all and use feedback and critique to ensure that children can progress and succeed.
- We give pupils time and opportunity to respond to critique and improve their skills.

Mastery

We believe that all pupils can master key knowledge and skills.

- Our curriculum is designed so that all children are given the opportunities and time needed to master objectives.
- *Teaching structures allow for extra support or challenge where needed.*
- *Strong assessment for learning in every classroom ensures that all children can be given precise and direct instruction and overcome any barriers to mastery.*
- We allow each child time to practise skills until they become ingrained – as a craftsman or sportsman would do – and this includes opportunities to redraft and edit work to achieve excellence.
- All children are explicitly encouraged to develop stamina in their learning.

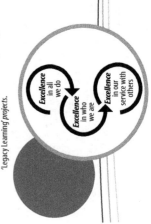

34

Excellence as Standard at St Peter's

Experts

We can all learn from others who are experts in their field – artists, sportspeople, writers or musicians. They inspire us to develop our own skills and knowledge in order to achieve our own excellence. *We recognise that becoming an 'expert' takes practice and resilience but everyone has the capacity to become an expert in time.*

- We provide opportunities for children and staff to engage with a range of experts and draw on their skills and knowledge to support their own learning. *We seek to involve experts from our parents and local community wherever we can.*
- *We know that all experts were once novices and we will all make mistakes on our journey to becoming experts.*
- We give children opportunities to act as experts and share this with their peers.
- When appropriate, we gain external verification from organisations to recognise our expertise and skills.

Models and Clarity

Models give us a clear understanding of what we are aiming to achieve. Alongside these, learners need clarity to ensure they know the steps they need to be successful.

- Staff and children use WAGOLLs (what a good one looks like) to show examples of what we are trying to achieve.
- Staff have clarity about what they are teaching and children are clear about how this fits into their bigger learning journey as well as understanding the smaller steps they are making.
- We identify and break down the steps or process that is needed to achieve the end goal.

Active ingredients: A School Culture of Excellence is...

- Having ethics and values that compel students to achieve more than they think is possible.

- Creating a peer culture that values academic effort and achievement – safe to care, cool to care.

- Knowing that communities matter – that is where the power rests. They must feel seen and valued.

- A clean and well-kept school. It is a message – a visual model of the school's ethic of excellence.

- Understanding that there are no shortcuts to creating a School Culture of Excellence. It is a long-term commitment. It is a way of life.

References.

Allison, S. and Tharby, A. (2015) *Making every lesson count.* Wales: Crown House Publishing.

Bambrick-Santoyo, P. (2018) *Leverage Leadership 2.0: A practical guide to building exceptional schools.* San Francisco, USA: Jossey-Bass, p. 201.

Bennett, T. (2017) *Creating a culture: How school leaders can optimise behaviour.* London: Department for Education.

Coates, M. (2017) 'Coping with rapid change.' In: Sage, R. (ed.) *Paradoxes in Education.* Rotterdam: Sense Publishers.

Cremin, T., Mottram, M., Collins, F. M., Powell, S. and Drury, R. (2004) *Researching literacy lives: Building communities between home and school.* Abingdon: Routledge.

Ford, D. and Wolfe, A. (n. d.) *Called, connected, committed: Leadership practices for educational leaders.* The Church of England Foundation for Educational Leadership.

Fritzgerald, A. (2020) *Antiracism and universal design for learning: Building expressways to success.* Massachusetts, USA: CAST Inc.

Gonzalez, N., Moll, L. C. and Amanti, C. (eds.) (2005) *Funds of knowledge: Theorising practices in households, communities and classrooms.* Marwah NJ: Lawrence Erlbaum Associates.

Hammond, Z. (2015) *Culturally responsive teaching and the brain: Promoting authentic engagement and rigor among culturally and linguistically diverse students.* USA: Corwin, Sage.

Myatt, M. (2016) *High challenge, low threat: Finding the balance.* Woodbridge: John Catt Educational Ltd.

National Equity Project. (n. d.) Available at: www.nationalequityproject.org/education-equity-definition (Accessed: 16 December 2021).

Stefanini, L. and Griffiths, J. (2020) *Addressing the challenges of using evidence in education.* Available at: https://impact.chartered.college/article/addressing-the-challenges-using-evidence-education/ (Accessed: 21 December 2021).

Watson, N. (2001) 'Promising practices: What does it really take to make a difference?' *Education Canada*, 40(4): pp. 4-6. www.edglossary.org/school-culture/

# CHAPTER 3

THE SECOND TOOLBOX: WORK OF EXCELLENCE

SECTION 1: MODELS – TRACEY ADAMS

Source: Sherrington and Caviglioli (2020) Teaching WalkThrus: Five-step guides to instructional coaching.

> 'No amount of words can convey
> what one good model tells me … I want my students to carry
> around pictures in their head of quality work.'
> ### Ron Berger

In his opening paragraphs, Berger details how as an apprentice builder he was trained by a master carpenter, who taught him his craft not through endless explanations but through modelling and examples. Berger stated that, 'No amount of words could convey what one good model taught me. I carried around that vision in my head and I always knew what I was striving for.' As Berger stated when feeding back on this section, 'I would add that models from the professional world are also very valuable. If students look at work from Andy Goldsworthy or Eric Carle, for example. There is almost nothing more needed to get kids inspired to do beautiful things. And when students read a strong book review or scientific journal article, they know what the real world expects for those genres.'

This resonated with me, as it exposed the idea that quality modelling gives students an example of excellence. An example that they can carry around with them; something they can visualise and make sense of, using it as a support to help construct their own model of exemplary work. Berger's thoughts on modelling are exciting and they align very closely to what is explored in the Education Endowment Foundation's (EEF) guidance report on metacognition and self-regulated learning (2018). The report lists seven recommendations for developing metacognitively deft learners. Recommendation three focuses on the idea that modelling is the cornerstone of effective teaching. It reveals the thought processes, and I would add the movements of an expert learner, which if harnessed, can help to develop our students' metacognitive skills. The report goes on to say, that when teachers scaffold tasks and share worked examples, they give space for students to develop their own model of excellence, without putting too much cognitive load on their mental resources. By revealing the task and the strategies, you give them space to move on from a place of understanding what excellence entails and what the end product could look like – taking them from the place of a novice to that of an expert.

Like Berger, the guidance report ties their explanation of modelling with a profession; this time it is a tailor, working with his/her apprentice. 'A tailor will teach an apprentice by allowing them to work alongside them, watching their movements and techniques closely, modelling their craft. The most effective teachers – like a master craftsman working with a novice apprentice – are aware of their expertise and of how to reveal their skills to learners.' These expert craftsmen and teachers are aware of the purpose of modelling. They know that modelling is a chance to leave an imprint of excellence in an apprentice or pupil's mind, which will help them to work more independently and think metacognitively.

Tom Sherrington (2017) supports this idea, when he states: 'It is powerful to show students how you approach tasks yourself; you show them how it is done. There's no point talking in theoretical abstract terms when you can provide an example and walk through it.' As educators, the moment we engage in modelling, we have to see it as a chance to do something really powerful for our students. We have a chance to leave them with an expert model; a chance to make the abstract concrete and support their conceptual understanding of a complex process.

This body of work we share with our students can be seen as exemplars: carefully chosen samples of student (and I would include the teacher's) work used to illustrate dimensions of quality. This is more than just a list of steps to follow, examples or a set of techniques. It needs to be something they can admire, something they can be inspired by and most of all, something they can engage with by analysing/reflecting on both its strengths and weaknesses. This step of analytical thinking is a key part of the modelling process, as it gets to the heart of why this model of excellence is so good. This idea of reflecting and critiquing is explored by Adam Lawrence (2020), who states: 'Exploring a model paragraph and dissecting it is gold dust for students who want to close the gap between novice and expert and to be able to articulate their own arguments beyond the scholarly wisdom of others.'

This idea of analysing is explored further by Sadler (2010). He states that 'the analysis of exemplars is a potentially powerful way of familiarising students with academic standards and supporting them to make informed evaluative judgements.' It gives them a chance to pull out the strengths of a piece, its weakness and look at how the exemplars could even be improved. This opportunity to judge and appraise a model can yield a number of important wins for teachers:

1. Clarity of expectations and standards; enabling students to develop an evolving sense of what good work looks like.
2. Enhanced capacities to make sound evaluative judgements, within their own work and across their peers.
3. Potentially improving learning outcomes; it can be seen as a high-leverage strategy.

An example of analysing a model in English

As part of the modelling process, Berger encourages his students to copy the models of excellence they are presented with. He calls this tribute work and defines it as 'the work of a student who has built off, borrowed ideas from or imitated the work of a particular student.' In his classroom space, this is not looked upon as cheating or copying but acknowledged as a legitimate and wise step on his pupils' journey to creating exemplary work.

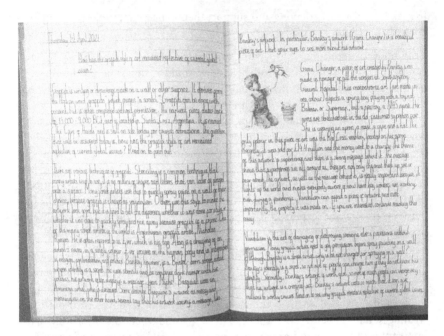

This idea of tributary work is an important stage on the journey from novice to expert, and links closely to the idea of gradual release theory. The gradual release of responsibility model provides teachers with an instructional framework for moving from teacher knowledge to student understanding and application. The gradual release of responsibility ensures that students are supported in their acquisition of the skills and strategies necessary for success.

The idea of gradual release is embedded within the EEF's seven-step planning model. The model reveals that over time there should be a release from teacher to student and this gives students a chance to go from dependence to independence.

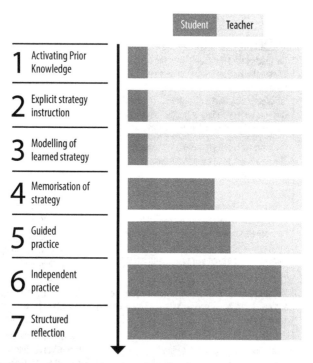

Source: EEF (2018) Metacognition and self-regulated learning: Guidance report.

Active ingredients: Modelling is...

- An opportunity to provide students with excellent examples of work.
- Giving children time and support to analyse the strengths and weaknesses of an exemplar. What makes this work strong?
- Saving models of the final product and also models of earlier drafts, so that students can see both the creative and refinement processes.
- Encouraging students to practise, using the model as a guide.
- Keeping a wide range of models, so that students do not think there is only one response to a particular question, task or problem.

Curriculum examples – models		
Subject	**Example**	**Think questions**
Maths	The teacher uses the exemplar to show the step-by-step thinking involved in understanding a mathematical concept. The teacher then uses the exemplar to start a discussion to further the students understanding of the mathematical concept and accompanying procedures.	• How could you use exemplars to support students to create their own procedural steps and mathematical representations?
Art	The art teacher can set the excellence bar by showing the class an exceptional piece of artwork created by an artist or a previous student.	• How could you use exemplars to support students to create their own steps for success and next steps?
Science	The teacher models the complete ideal written response to a biology, chemistry or physics question. The model is used to take students from their prior knowledge and develop and guide them into deeper, conceptual understanding. The students use the exemplar to guide their responses during independent practice.	• How will the exemplar support students to demonstrate knowledge of the science being taught? • What do you want students to be able to write during their independent work?
PE	Models are used to enable the deliberate practice and development of specific skills. They are used across a variety of sports and games. This could include: • Catching, jumping and throwing. • Swimming. • Tactics within a team sport. • Performing specific movements and balances.	• What question will the teacher ask students to enable them to reflect on and practice what they have seen? • How will the responses enable the students to confidently apply and assess the skills independently and across disciplines? • As students progress, how will the models enable more complex thinking and collaboration?

References.

EEF. (2018) *Metacognition and self-regulated learning: Guidance report.* Available at: https://educationendowmentfoundation.org.uk/education-evidence/guidance-reports/metacognition (Accessed: 16 December 2021).

Lawrence, A. (2020) *More effective teaching through modelling. Impact* – Journal of the Chartered College of Teaching.

Sadler, D. R. (2010) 'Beyond feedback: Developing student capability in complex appraisal.' Assessment & Evaluation in Higher Education, 35(5): pp. 535-550.

Sherrington, T. (2017) *The learning rainforest.* Woodbridge: John Catt Educational Ltd.

SECTION 2: MULTIPLE DRAFTS – DANIEL MARTIN

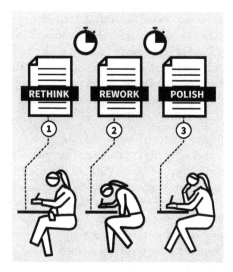

Source: Sherrington and Caviglioli (2020) Teaching WalkThrus: Five-step guides to instructional coaching.

'What could you produce of quality in a single draft?'

Ron Berger

Prior to embarking on the clamorous journey that is 'multiple drafts', it is expedient for both the practitioner and the learner to explore 'the why'. In an educational climate that seemingly values quantity over quality, seldom do we take the time to explore why we do what we do. Drafting on multiple occasions is something that certainly has the potential to be negated or continue to be neglected if we have not defined the purpose of it for our own context.

We are all familiar with the age-old adage 'Rome wasn't built in a day'. Ron Berger poses a question that is rooted in the same spirit: 'What could you produce of quality in a single draft?' Whether consciously or subconsciously, this is a question that continues to echo in the mind of any practitioner who desires the very best outcomes for the students that they teach. The simple answer to this question is nothing, nothing at all can be produced in a single draft, which is considered to be of quality. The essence of the excellence achieved in Austin's Butterfly is 'drafting on multiple occasions'.

45

Let us first consider what drafting is and why it is necessary to draft in order to achieve a quality piece of work. While drafting in the context of written composition refers to the process of generating preliminary versions of a written work, it is important to remember that drafting can, and in fact should, happen at any stage of the writing process. Every teacher, leader and educational setting ought to flee from the notion that drafting is an event that takes place once students have finished writing. Drafting should be taking place even prior to the writing process. It should be commonplace for students to also rework and adapt at the planning stage.

In fact, Ron Berger states, 'Students need to know from the outset that quality means rethinking, reworking, and polishing. They need to feel that they will be celebrated, not ridiculed, for going back to the drawing board.' Drafting should be viewed as a developmental process and inextricably tied to the editing process. The Education Endowment Foundation makes this progressive relationship clear in their series of guidance documents aimed at improving literacy from the early years foundation stage up to the secondary key stages. Berger's thought is supported by recommendation five of the key stage 1 EEF literacy guidance: 'Encouraging children to manage and monitor aspects of their writing is a key step ... Drafting, revising and editing – helping pupils to get their ideas written down as a first draft which they can then edit and revise.'

This is all likely to raise questions and possible concerns among teachers, such as 'How long will all of this take?', 'This all seems very long winded' or 'There isn't enough time to do this.' However, these concerns can be addressed with a simple question: what do you want your students to produce – excellence or mediocrity?

Not only can quality not be produced in a single draft, but it also cannot be produced in haste. Of course, we must remain time conscious, but it should not be at the expense of producing quality. So, let us first acknowledge that redrafting is time-consuming, but it is also necessary to allow time for works of excellence to be produced.

Producing multiple drafts does come with a warning to avoid the potential of what Kalyuga refers to as the 'expertise reversal effect' (2009), which can be a hindrance to the children in your class with a greater level of expertise. For example, if your higher attainers will not benefit from reproducing their entire publications, then it would be expedient to avoid doing so.

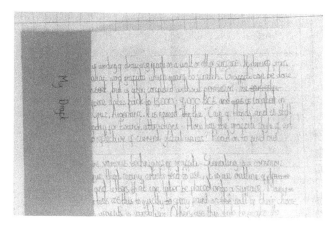

Another reason to retain every phase of the drafting process is to support the process of curating a set of exemplars. There is no shortage of exemplification materials available to teaching practitioners, but what better exemplars to have than those produced by your own students! The collection of exemplars is not something that practitioners will need to frantically search for or labour intensively to create; on the contrary – exemplars will be a natural by-product of the quality work that has been produced as a result of drafting on multiple occasions.

Guide student practice

Barak Rosenshine highlights a number of principles of instruction and while many of them are applicable to teaching students how to effectively draft, there is one principle in particular that will help the children to develop a strong and robust schema and that is principle number five: guiding student practice. How is this applicable to multiple drafts and why is it not only relevant but necessary? While there is still a conversation to be had regarding the place of 'discovery learning', the research is clear that for novices (the children who make up the bulk of our classrooms) fully guided teacher instruction is far more efficacious than a lack of instruction.

'Teachers can model their thinking as they approach a task to reveal the reflections of an effective learner' (EEF, 2018). Just like every other phase of the writing process, the success of the learner and quality of the outcomes often hinges on the quality of the instruction and model that is provided. It is therefore imperative that drafting is taught explicitly and, when guiding learners, the practitioner has a golden opportunity to expose how they think as a writer.

This guided process gives the practitioner the chance to home in on a select group of children and address sticking points within the drafting process. The guided group may be where you choose to: evaluate a previous piece (deciding what to keep, take away and refine); focus on a particular section (typically something that affects the group); and provide further models and worked examples. This is where the teacher really is able to build on the existing schema that children possess. According to the Centre for Education Statistics and Evaluation (CESE), 'Schemas provide a number of important functions that are relevant to learning. First, they provide a system for organising and storing knowledge. Second, and crucially for cognitive load theory, they reduce working memory load. This is because, although there are a limited number of elements that can be held in working memory at one time, a schema constitutes only a single element in working memory' (CESE, 2017).

To avoid the process of multiple drafting feeling like a waste of time, it is important that the students are taught to understand that there is a need to redraft. Purpose is a prerequisite to excellence, so if there is a genuine need to redraft and the student has been shown what it is that needs to be improved then ideally, they will be the one to suggest redrafting. This will only happen once the student has been exposed to guided sessions, shown effective models and had a chance to collaborate with both their peers and their teachers.

Encourage collaboration

According to Paul Black and Dylan Wiliam (2010), 'Feedback to any pupil should be about the particular qualities of his or her work, with advice on what he or she can do to improve and should avoid comparisons with other pupils.'

This was demonstrated so beautifully in the video that we see of Austin's Butterfly – a plethora of friendly yet useful critique from a group of children, which was carefully tempered by the adult.

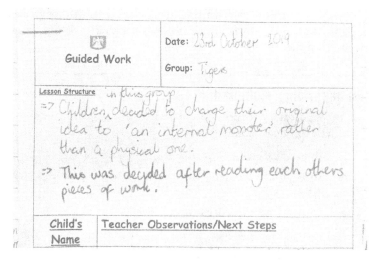

| Guided Work | Date: 23rd October 2019 |
| | Group: Tigers |

Lesson Structure *in this group*

=> Children decided to change their original idea to 'an internal monster' rather than a physical one.

=> This was decided after reading each others pieces of work.

Child's Name	Teacher Observations/Next Steps

This lies at the heart of multiple drafting – it is both peer-to-peer and teacher-to-child interactions that bring about rich discourse, critique and recommendations. Ron Berger suggests three simple rules when critiquing a student's work:

- Be kind.
- Be specific.
- Be helpful.

Of course, ensuring kind feedback from peers is something that is birthed out of a classroom and school environment that lives this daily and is a genuine cultural norm for the school. The specificity of the critique is an element that will need to be modelled, taught and developed over time in order for students to identify the minutiae details that will in turn be helpful to their peers. Drafting is a collaborative effort and shouldn't be done in isolation even for those who are able to do so independently. According to Berger, 'The truth is this: If my house had a list of credits like those that appear at the end of a movie, it would be a long list. At this point I can't even remember which ideas were mine and which came from my son, my electrician, my building partners.'

'Writing can be thought of as a process made up of seven components. Pupils should be taught each of these components and underlying strategies. A strategy is a series of actions that writers use to achieve their goals and may support one or more components of the writing process. Strategies should be carefully modelled and practised. Drafting – focusing on noting down key ideas. Pupils should set out their writing in a logical order. Although accurate spelling, grammar and handwriting are important, at this stage they are not the main focus' (EEF, 2021).

Active ingredients: Multiple drafts are...

- An opportunity to provide children with the time to draft and redraft (produce multiple drafts)
  - To produce quality.
  - To fulfil the on-going element of the writing process, which requires time.
  - To avoid the 'expertise reversal effect'.

- A chance to keep evidence of each stage of drafting
  - For evidence of teaching and learning.
  - For evidence of assessment.
  - For exemplars (only the exceptional publications).
  - For models (used during the drafting process).

- A guide for student practice
  - Through fully guided instruction.
  - Through review.
  - Through critique (gallery and in-depth).

- A way of encouraging collaboration
  - Peer to peer.
  - Through teacher (expert) to child (novice).

Curriculum examples – multiple drafts		
Subject	Example	Think questions
Maths	Teachers can use multiple drafts to support students to iteratively evolve and revise their written mathematical responses. As their thinking shifts with each draft, they move closer to the final solution.	• How can we use multiple drafts to support students' mathematical thinking? • How can we use multiple drafts to support students' mathematical reasoning? • How can we use multiple drafts to support students' problem solving? • How can you use multiple drafts to deepen students' verbal and written responses?
Art	Museum visits, artist visits/videos and case studies are used to define what excellence looks like throughout the multiple drafts and motivate students to strive for improvements.	• How can we support students to use feedback from teachers and peers to aid each stage of the drafting process?

References.

Black, P. and Wiliam, D. (2010) 'Inside the black box: Raising standards through classroom assessment.' *Phi Delta Kappan*, 92(1): pp. 81-90.

CESE. (2017) *Cognitive load theory: Research that teachers really need to understand.* Available at: https://havelockprimaryschool.com/wp-content/uploads/2018/11/cognitive-load-theory-VR_AA3.pdf (Accessed: 13 January 2022).

EEF. (2018) *Metacognition and self-regulated learning: Guidance report.* Available at: https://educationendowmentfoundation.org.uk/education-evidence/guidance-reports/metacognition (Accessed: 17 December 2021).

EEF. (2020) *Improving literacy in key stage 1: Guidance report.* Available at: https://educationendowmentfoundation.org.uk/education-evidence/guidance-reports/literacy-ks-1 (Accessed: 16 December 2021).

EEF. (2021) *Improving literacy in key stage 2: Guidance report.* Available at: https://educationendowmentfoundation.org.uk/education-evidence/guidance-reports/literacy-ks2 (Accessed: 13 January 2022).

Kalyuga, S. (2009) *Managing cognitive load in adaptive multimedia learning.* London: IGI Global.

SECTION 3: CRITIQUE – HYDEH FAYAZ

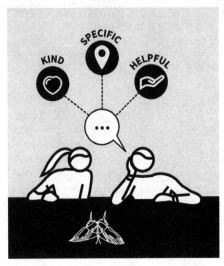

Source: Sherrington and Caviglioli (2020) Teaching WalkThrus: Five-step guides to instructional coaching.

'I suggest teachers take critique to a whole new level and make critique a habit of the mind that suffuses the classroom in all subjects.'

Ron Berger

Ron Berger beautifully summarises his belief in this quote. A belief that makes the *Toolbox: Work of Excellence* a must-have for classroom practitioners – they must carry this toolbox with them everywhere, if you will. In our classrooms, the word critique must be disassociated with negative connotations. The act itself harnesses power. Power to create amazing work. Power to drive intrinsic motivation. Power to drive improvement. When critique is explicitly taught and is understood, enacted and welcomed by the pupils, craftsmanship is truly in progress.

In the second toolbox 'Work of Excellence' Berger takes the reader on a journey of how critique has transformed his pupils and their motivation to produce a piece of excellence no matter the project at hand. This toolbox came to life in my Year 5 classroom. The aim was for children to read with fluency and perform to a high standard so we could win the prestigious CLiPPA poetry Shadowing Scheme (a scheme that aims to promote the teaching of poetry in schools). Embarking on this project was necessary for several reasons; the poems by Karmelo C. Iribarren (translated by Lawrence Schimel) were a must-read; I wanted to improve my children's fluency in reading; and the critique in my class was often teacher to student or peer on peer – I wanted to introduce a group endeavour.

Children critiquing each other to achieve their collective aim
Why fluency?
As stated by Rasinski in *The Megabook of Fluency* (2018):

'The research of the past two decades demonstrates quite clearly a robust correlation between expressive oral reading and silent reading comprehension.'

This silent reading comprehension is what I wanted to develop. If children can learn to read in their heads as they are expected to read aloud (with expression, intonation and overall prosody) then their comprehension will improve. Authentic fluency (real reading of real texts for a real reason) leads to higher levels of reading proficiency, including comprehension, greater levels of interest and motivation for reading.

Authentic fluency is a daily endeavour at St Matthew's through story time – a daily *happy place* that is enough to maintain momentum. The CLiPPA Shadowing Scheme enhanced this authentic platform. The contest was shared through our reading for pleasure session (fortnightly sessions) and within a matter of moments, children had selected a poem that resonated with them the most. With that, they formed their groups.

Critique

'The ultimate goal of critique is to share knowledge and skills.'
Ron Berger

Through looking at students' work carefully, we unlock improvement for all. We create metacognitive learners who become aware of strategies and then deliberately use them which makes work excellent. Dylan Wiliam suggests, 'The most successful learners attribute both successes and failures to internal, unstable, specific factors: it's down to them (internal) and they can do something about it (unstable).'

The emphasis is on the child as the catalyst for improvement. Through critique, they understand that their learning and understanding is not fixed, it develops. Critique makes the children aware of these processes; it makes them metacognitive.

Metacognitive learners who can control and monitor their cognition, metacognition and emotions lead to self-regulated learners who can 'activate and sustain cognitions, behaviours systematically oriented towards the attainment of their learning goals'. Critiquing each other's poetry performances seemed personal at first, but a key element of this toolbox is to use I statements: 'I felt scared when you used hushed tones reading that line.'

This small tweak to our critique ensured the focus was on the audience and how we made them feel; that was, after all, what would make us successful in this task. In order for these skills to transfer, children were prompted to identify when we were using key skills in our reading lessons, story times, history lessons etc. Coming back to my original aim: feedback is used not to look backwards, not to just improve the work but to improve the learner.

What is the process?

In order to cultivate learners such as this, we need to start roots-first and ensure that the conditions in the classroom are right. In Year 5, *our culture is to improve* and the children must have the language in order to self-regulate their learning so *we know how to improve*. Carrying out in-depth critique and gallery critiques are the two formats Berger uses in his classroom. Children becoming self-regulated learners as outlined by Zimmerman are 'proactive in their efforts to learn because they are aware of their strengths and limitations and because they are guided by personally set goals and task-related strategies'.

There were two goals for critiquing the way children read:

1. To improve their comprehension strategies.
2. To win the competition!

While the latter was an extrinsic motivator, the intrinsic belief to be better at reading was the driver. Activating each other to improve ensured that at the point of reading, fluency was what we were thinking about.

Creating habit of the mind

> 'In the heat of a good critique, we may abandon guidelines, but we never abandon [norms].'

> 'If learners have no interest in improvement then no matter how thoughtful and insightful the feedback is, the time that teachers spend on crafting [it] is likely to be wasted.'

> **Ron Berger**

Creating the right conditions and environment for learning to thrive needs consistency over a period of time. Creating the right environment to equalise pupils speaking opportunities requires *norms*. It is these norms that teachers should prioritise at the beginning of each academic year. Doing this means children know that their voices are to be heard and they in turn understand that their voices are respected – a fundamental part of creating a 'culture of excellence'. These norms for classroom talk then become 'routinised' through reinforcement and use which is necessary because children do not intuitively know how to work together. We need to leverage these in order to secure motivation.

Creating this environment is done through dialogic principles. As teachers, we facilitate that talk which is supportive and enables students to express ideas freely, without risk of embarrassment over contributions that are hesitant or tentative. They can help each other reach common understandings.

For our pupils to habitually think in a certain way, we need to explicitly teach this. Pupils will engage in this habit once they have felt successful. As McCrea (2020) states, 'The more successful we have been in the past, the more likely we are to invest in similar opportunities in the future.' The concept that students have their own abilities and worth is shaped by their classroom experiences, especially their interactions with other students.

In *The Hidden Lives of Learners*, Graham Nuthall (2007) suggests that a learner evaluating their understanding (which takes place in working memory) is of the 'validity of the learner themselves against their peers'. So our purpose is to develop a culture of mutual respect and co-operation within the classroom. Relationship triggers prevent our students from taking the advantage of the available feedback to improve their capabilities. Students need to have trust that whoever is providing the critique is the expert and will make moves and feedback provisions in order for them to improve.

As Wiliam suggests: 'The curious task of teachers is to work towards their own redundancy' so pupils can act as excellent role models for each other. In order for this to happen we have to model feedback which should be:

- Specific and clear – reflect: does my feedback have an aim?
- Focused on the task – reflect: will it work to improve the learner in the task they are engaged with?
- Explanatory.
- Designed to attribute outcomes to factors students can control – reflect: is the feedback amenable to change? If students are unable to act on the feedback, then will they ever be able to provide it to a peer?

- Designed to link outcomes and efforts – reflect: do I inform pupils, 'If you do x then y will happen'?

I did wonder about those children for whom performing or reading fluently comes naturally. What about their development? What could their peers possibly offer children who read with prosody that rivals mine? Slavin, Hurley and Chamberlain (2003) state there are four mechanisms by which group-based activities could increase learning, all but one of which benefits high achievers.

1.   Positive interdependence.
2.   Care about the group.
3.   Individual needs are met more frequently (by pupils and teacher).
4.   Cognitive elaboration.

If we frame the feedback as a defining feature of the group – 'In this class, we all push each other, because we care about everyone getting better' – then we provide status for children and make them feel like they belong.

Powerful projects with a purpose

> 'It may sound obvious ... have assignments that inspire and challenge students ... there's only so much care that a student can put into filling in the blanks on a worksheet.'
>
> **Ron Berger**

It certainly sounds obvious but is sadly all too infrequent, in many classrooms. We need to motivate our pupils and ensure they invest their motivation. Peps McCrea (2020) states that 'motivation governs both our initial choice and ongoing effort' vital for a team endeavour to be successful.

So if pupils attach value to tasks it means they have conscious or subconscious thoughts such as 'What could the benefits be if we invest our attention here, both to us as an individual and to our groups?' While we are unable to enter poetry competitions every day, it is clear that leaders and teachers must think wisely about the true purpose and audience of children's work. Teachers who understand the importance of motivation provide children with a rationale why. This in turn makes their investment more secure. Thinking about motivation as a specific response rather than a general trait of a child is a truly important nuance for schools to become accustomed with.

All of the above is with the aim of creating metacognitive learners.

Powerful project was a seamless transition from everyday classroom practice to an authentic purpose to critique.

Establishing specific critique to create a metalanguage

'Once they learn the vocabulary that describes the dimensions of the work, they are often clear about exactly what impresses them.'

Ron Berger

'Careful groundwork before the feedback is given, providing well-timed information that focuses on improvement, and also taking into account how learners receive and use that information.'

EEF (2021)

To give critique that was precise, the children needed to know the metalanguage required to improve a performance of a prosodic read. Pre-teaching this vocabulary was vital. It allowed us to optimise intrinsic load because 'new vocabulary is a common source of high cognitive load for students'. This meant that when pupils were watching their group or each other to critique them, they could listen to the words, look at the body language, and think about tonal variation rather than think 'How am I going to critique this?' To begin this process, the key tier three terminology was defined through explicit instruction. Through the use of activities in Isabel Beck et al. (2013) *Bringing Words to Life*, the words, the parameters of use, examples and non-examples were explored. As these words are transferable, because reading (fluent reading!) is a condition of learning, there was ample opportunity to recall and retrieve what *intonation* sounded like, or how automaticity affects the audience's comprehension of what is being read aloud. This meant that the terminology used by the children did not remain abstract, but instead it was a concrete experience they lived day in, day out. The language was applied in our fluency interventions (weekly) and shared and guided reading lessons as well as in children's performance time.

Pre-teaching vocabulary is something we all do (tier two words in novels, tier three words in science) but how often do we teach vocabulary and structures that allow for improvement? 'You used x which made me feel y.'

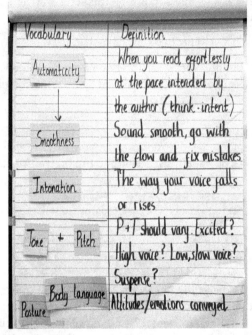

Vocabulary	Definition
Automaticity ↓	When you read effortlessly at the pace intended by the author (think - intent)
Smoothness	Sound smooth, go with the flow and fix mistakes
Intonation	The way your voice falls or rises
Tone + Pitch	P + T should vary. Excited? High voice? Low, slow voice? Suspense?
Posture, Body language	Attitudes / emotions conveyed

Through the understanding of this terminology, we were able to refine our idea of what constitutes an excellent performance. We applied a 'gallery critique' lens to poet performances. What was it about their performance that made it worthy of a win? This act moved beyond the *expert competence* and the *curse of knowledge* and modelled the implicit thinking that creates natural expertise. This enabled us to build our own success criteria for our performances, linked to how to engage an audience and project your voice. To firm up assessment, we linked this to the Oracy Skills Framework (Oracy Cambridge, 2019). This enabled some level of standardisation and measurable outcome but also left space for conveying meaning and a level of interpretation.

This 'powerful project with a purpose' reached an outstanding conclusion when St Matthew's were declared the overall winners of the 2021 CLiPPA Shadowing Scheme.

Case study

Kate Jones is head of history at The British School Al Khubairat, Abu Dhabi, author of the *Retrieval Practice* collection and *In Action: Wiliam and Leahy's Five Formative Assessment Strategies*. Kate tweets @KateJones_teach.

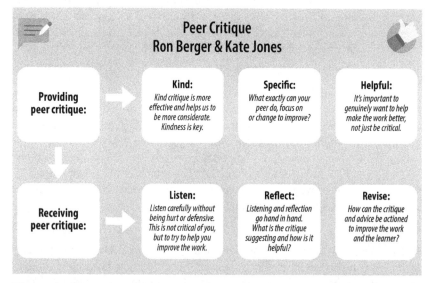

The work of Ron Berger has had a significant impact on my classroom practice. Providing critique that is kind, specific and helpful has become well known across many schools but just as important, arguably more so, is how students respond and act on the critique and feedback provided.

In addition to Berger, many other leading voices in education such as Dylan Wiliam and John Hattie have stressed the importance of students responding to any critique and feedback they receive. Critique can be kind and specific but if students choose to ignore it, then it won't be helpful.

I reached out to Ron Berger to ask for advice and he helped me to create the graphic above. I wanted to create a graphic that included kind, specific and helpful but took that a step further with advice as to how students should receive feedback. Naturally, we cannot and should not tell students how to respond to the critique they receive but we can offer advice and guidance, encouraging students to embrace rather than dismiss or ignore critique. After careful consideration and acting on the generous advice from Berger, I decided to include and focus on *listen, reflect and revise*.

Listen

Listening has to be the first part of the process when receiving critique and feedback. Professor John Hattie profoundly stated, 'If feedback falls in a classroom and no one hears it, did it make a sound?' Listening is absolutely essential in a classroom, whether that be the student listening to the teacher, the teacher listening to their students or peers listening to each other. The aim of peer critique is for students to support one another and learn from one another; this cannot be achieved if they don't listen to each other.

Reflect

Teachers recognise the power of reflection, as this is something we constantly do to improve and develop our practice. Students also need to grasp and understand the power of reflection. As stated above, listening and reflection go hand in hand. Listening without reflection is more akin to hearing critique rather than understanding and responding to critique. Do students actually know how to reflect on their work and critique provided? As teachers we need to model this and have explicit conversations about what reflection looks like and how it can have a positive impact.

Revise

The final element is to revise their original piece of work. Once students have listened to and reflected on the critique they should know how to act on that. If the critique has been kind, specific and helpful then the students should know how they act on that critique to improve the specific piece of work as well as improving in the future. As Dylan Wiliam often notes we should focus on improving the learner, not the work. Improving the work should be a result of the learner improving by acting on critique and feedback.

Case study

Jamie Clark began his career in the UK as an English teacher and lead practitioner. Since moving to Australia in 2015, Jamie has become a team leader responsible for research, coaching and CPD at his school, Mother Teresa Catholic College in Perth. Jamie regularly shares evidence-informed practice on twitter @XpatEducator. His resources and ideas are made freely available to educators.

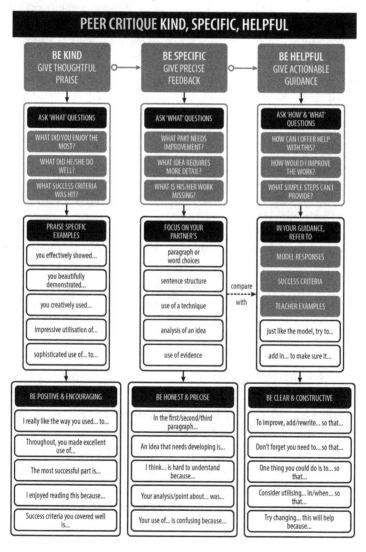

I was passionate about creating a culture of critique, where students aim for and celebrate excellence. I think Berger's kind, specific and helpful framework helps to scaffold this mindset for students. I developed mine to support English teachers, as crafting and drafting is a big part of the writing process.

Our teachers encourage students to aim for excellence and have a mindset in which they are never satisfied with less. To help develop a culture of critique, we rely on formative feedback strategies and dedicate time for students to craft their work so that they are able to make small improvements. This means that all work set has to be meaningful and challenging.

Teachers often conduct 'gallery critique' exercises so that students are able to see a broad scope of work (varying in quality) and offer measured feedback. Students are familiar with constructive 'critique language' and use post-it notes to jot down 'kind, specific and helpful' comments based on co-constructed success criteria.

In recent months, we have developed word diagrams that serve as visual scaffolds to support learning. My peer critique word diagram maps out the feedback process step by step and provides students with guiding sentence starters. The diagram also prompts students to consult teacher samples, success criteria, and model answers to inform their feedback. Before engaging in peer critique exercises, teachers always reiterate the process by explaining each step of the diagram section by section.

Being an iPad school means that our students use hybrid learning apps like Showbie to digitally record audio feedback on sample work. This unobtrusive use of technology is not only a time saver, but helps to students to verbalise 'kind, specific and helpful' language so that it is normalised and becomes a habit.

At my school, we have worked hard to make the ethic of excellence a key part of our whole-school CPD models and day-to-day pedagogy through:

- CPD cycles with strands dedicated to feedback and critique.
- Instructional coaching and observations to develop practical approaches to feedback.
- Informal opportunities for teachers to share strategies (teacher spotlights and '15 Minute Forums').
- Resource creation (such as word diagrams) to scaffold critique activities.

- Explicit teaching and rehearsal of critique language (using 'kind, specific and helpful' sentence starters).
- Technology integrated meaningfully for audio recorded feedback.

The next step for us is to establish channels for our students to present their work publicly. Showcasing work to an authentic audience helps to give students a sense of pride and celebrate their successes. As a technology-rich school, we are in a great position to promote the ethic of excellence digitally. In the near future, we intend to:

- Spotlight student work on e-boards displayed around the school.
- Publish interactive e-books featuring snap-shot samples of excellent work.
- Produce a Senior School, student-led podcast focusing on approaches to excellence.
- Feature stand-out students in a monthly newsletter emailed to the school community.

Active ingredients: Critique is...

- The culture of the classroom – it is the lesson.
- Name it to know it (in-depth critique and vocabulary).
- Powerful projects enabling intrinsic motivation.
- Metacognition – developing children's ability to know how they are improving.
- Teachers driving the critique culture in the room.

Curriculum examples – critique		
Subject	**Example**	**Think questions**
Drama	Students use videos of performance and theatre visits to create performances. Students are then asked to critique 'draft' performances of their devised pieces at the rehearsal stages. They repeat short performances, following feedback from peers and teachers.	• How can we support students to use the performance criteria to improve their own or their peers' performances through precise feedback?
MFL	Students translate a sentence/sentences from one language to another. They work with a peer to put post-it notes on each other's work, using grammatical metalanguage to support improvements.	• How can we use critique to enable students to identify grammatical and syntactical errors in their peer-translated sentences?
RE	Students develop their thinking through examining religious beliefs and teachings, and consider what questions need to be asked in order to understand them. They also examine whether their responses are valid. (Cox, 2015)	• How can questions be linked to reliability, credibility and logic of reasoning in order to deepen students' critical thinking? • How can developing children's critical thinking, through questionings and answers, enable students to embed this into their written responses?

References.

Beck, I., McKeown, M., and Kucan, L. (2013) *Bringing words to life: Robust vocabulary instruction.* New York: The Guildford Press.

Chiles, M. (2021) *The feedback pendulum: A manifesto for enhancing feedback in education.* Woodbridge: John Catt Educational.

Cox, D. (2015) *Critique in RE.* Blog. Available at: https://missdcoxblog.wordpress.com/2015/05/ (Accessed: 14 January 2022).

EEF. (2021) *Teacher feedback to improve pupil learning: Guidance report.* Available at: https://d2tic4wvo1iusb.cloudfront.net/eef-guidance-reports/feedback/Teacher_Feedback_to_Improve_Pupil_Learning.pdf (Accessed: 13 January 2022).

McCrea, P. (2020) *Motivated Teaching: Harnessing the science of motivation to boost attention and effort in the classroom* (High Impact Teaching Book 3). CreateSpace Independent Publishing Platform.

Nuthall, G. (2007) *The hidden lives of learners.* NZCER Press.

Oracy Cambridge. (2019) *The oracy skills framework and glossary.* Available at: https://oracycambridge.org/wp-content/uploads/2020/06/The-Oracy-Skills-Framework-and-Glossary.pdf (Accessed: 13 January 2022).

Rasinski, T. and Cheesman Smith, M. (2018) *The megabook of fluency.* USA: Scholastic.

Slavin, R. E., Hurley, E. A. and Chamberlain, A. (2003) 'Cooperative learning and achievement: Theory and research.' ResearchGate.

Wiliams, D. (2011) *Embedded formative assessment*. USA: Solution Tree Press.

Zimmerman, B. J. (2002) 'Becoming a self-regulated learner: An overview.' *Theory into Practice*, 41(2): pp. 64-70.

SECTION 4: MAKING WORK PUBLIC – SONIA THOMPSON

Source: Sherrington and Caviglioli (2020) Teaching WalkThrus: Five-step guides to instructional coaching.

'Not every project or assignment can have life importance, but when students know that their finished work will be displayed, presented, appreciated and judged – whether by the whole class, other classes, families or the community – work takes on a different meaning.'

Ron Berger

For Berger, making work public is about getting students to understand that there are times when their work will be seen by an audience of more than the teacher and the students' own class. On these occasions, they will have to put even more effort into what they are producing. It is about taking students' work beyond the singular audience and into a world where there is now even more of a reason to care about its quality.

Berger uses the term 'Arts' to encompass a range of opportunities, across various subjects and quotes Steve Seidel, who talks about the appeal of the aesthetic and this being a powerful driving force behind the accomplishments of cultures through history. Sherrington and Caviglioli (2021), call these powerful drivers 'hands on' and state, 'Numerous elements of a great knowledge-rich curriculum require students to gain knowledge first hand, through *hands-on* experiences: doing things, feeling things, experiencing things, seeing things for themselves.' They go on to say that these experiences cannot be left to chance. If they are planned then they are 'universal entitlements'.

Making work public at St Matthew's

At St Matthew's we are well on our way to creating at least two 'hands-on' experiences for our students across the year. One of these is our St Matthew's Art Gallery. The Gallery is the culmination of our Art and Design Week and provides an opportunity for parents to share in the excitement of seeing their child's work on display. This means that every child must have a piece that is worthy of display and it must be displayed with excellence.

For Berger, 'In addition to final products, displays of work may include drafts of earlier work, evidence of discussion, and the ideas and strategies involved in the work's creation.' For us, this is the children's art journals and curriculum books. We have a wonderful artist-in-residence at St Matthew's, so parents get a chance to see art skills and knowledge produced throughout the year.

Our teachers and teaching assistants put their hearts and souls into those displays. It is not just a reason to care for the students, it's a reason to care for us as well. Our aim is to create a real gallery experience and every year, when we finish, we step back and look around with a sense of genuine pride and love for what we do.

Making work public in other curriculum areas

English – publishing

The EEF guidance report *Improving Literacy in KS2* (2017) outlines the seven components of writing that pupils should be taught. The final one is 'Publishing: presenting the work so that others can read it. This may not be the outcome for all pieces of writing but when used appropriately it can provide a strong incentive for pupils to produce high quality writing and encourage them to carefully revise and edit. Example strategies: displaying work, presenting to other classes, and sending copies to parents and carers.'

Geography – audience-centred teaching

In his research, Butt (1998) explains audience-centred teaching as an 'attempt to involve children in talking to, and writing for, audiences different from the ones they would usually encounter in the geography classroom'. He unpicks how rather than producing their work solely for the 'teacher as assessor', children are emboldened to direct their written responses to individuals, or groups, beyond the classroom. Butt's research findings described in this paper suggest that by 'becoming more aware of their audiences, children can produce written work that is more personal and involving, and that, as a direct result, their understanding of geography may also improve'.

At St Matthew's we use whole-school assemblies to display acting skills, poetry, singing and dance. We also use other classes to display books created by classes. Other opportunities for display across the school include:

- A design and technology project where our students design, make, evaluate and display a hoodie.
- Tour guides, for the Shakespeare Trust.
- Christmas cantata.
- World Singing Day.
- Termly music concerts – involving all of our peripatetic musicians.
- CLiPPA awards (outlined in the critique section). Did I mention that we actually won! As part of the prize, our performers went to the Cheltenham Literature Festival and performed their poem to an audience of over 200 children and adults. Now that is making work public!

Berger finishes this section with such a sweet story about a new child to the school being asked how this school was different: '… she told them, in this school her work was public. Everyone looked at her work; everyone cared about her work … I have to try much harder in this school because the work is more important.' I wanted to end this section with a sweet story too. I got quite emotional when my IT technician said, 'I walked through the gallery and it was amazing. It gave me goosebumps.'

Active ingredients: Making work public is...

- An appreciation that sometimes children need more than the teacher as their audience. It doesn't have to be elaborate. Another class can be an audience.
- Publicly displaying children's work, so that it makes them feel it is valued and more important.
- Enabling children to care more when they have to present to others.
- An opportunity for children to articulate the challenges and victories that their work represents.
- A chance for the teachers to help children get their work ready to display… to a standard of excellence.

Curriculum examples – making work public		
Subject	**Example**	**Think questions**
All subjects	The school runs an excellence exhibition every year, from across the school or within the department. Parents and members of the community are invited to the event. Students are able to talk about their work and the thinking behind it.	• How can excellence exhibitions be planned to incentivise students, in all phases and stages?
All subjects	HODs/subject leaders use competitions from subject associations and other organisations (e.g. CLPE, STEM, Debate Mate, The Mathematical Association, Classics for All) or external exams (e.g. music, LAMDA) to motivate students to produce excellent work.	• How can we ensure all year groups have a least one different audience for their work (besides the class teacher)?

References.

Butt, G. (1998) 'Increasing the effectiveness of 'audience-centred' teaching in geography.' *International Research in Geographical and Environmental Education*, 7(3): pp. 203-218.

EEF. (2017) *Improving literacy in key stage 2: Guidance report.* Available at: https://educationendowmentfoundation.org.uk/education-evidence/guidance-reports/literacy-ks2 (Accessed: 13 January 2022).

Sherrington, T. and Caviglioli, O. (2021) *Teaching WalkThrus 2: Five-step guides to instructional coaching.* Woodbridge: John Catt Educational Ltd, p. 134.

CHAPTER 4

THE THIRD TOOLBOX: TEACHING OF EXCELLENCE

SONIA THOMPSON

'Builders receive guidance for years from the master builders. Teachers are left alone in the classroom … some struggle to develop systems and strategies … they often fall back on things that don't work … when forced to attend PD, they often talk about why things won't work.'

Ron Berger

Teaching as a calling

In this toolbox, Ron Berger could not be any clearer in his mandate that, 'If schools are to improve, it must begin here with the teachers.' He goes on to espouse that if, as a society, we cannot support teachers, then schools and education, no matter what governments do, will continue to deteriorate. This chimes with the Institute for Effective Teaching (2020), 'If nothing changes in the classroom, then nothing changes.' They go on to ask the question, 'How do teachers change, and hopefully improve, their practice, and what role does research evidence have in this?'

Before I look at this, let's go back to Berger. He is under no illusion that teaching is incredibly hard. He describes how it takes a level of endurance and tenacity which, for me, is often not respected or even understood by many of those outside the profession. Berger attributes the propensity for some teachers to do the job and do it well to the fact that for them, 'teaching is a calling'. These teachers are committed to doing everything they can to help their students to succeed because teaching is literally how, as Berger writes, 'they share the best of what they have to give to the world'.

In a way, this is what our school culture is built upon: the dogged determination to help our students to achieve beyond what they think is possible. For Berger, this 'calling' was made easier by being in a school that 'brought out the best in me' and 'shared a common vision that centered on the children'. He goes on to set out what schools need to do to recruit and keep talented and passionate teachers. What Berger is describing for me, is motivation. Sinclair (2008) defines teacher motivation in terms of attraction, retention and concentration and as something that determines 'what attracts individuals to teaching, how long they remain in their initial teacher education courses and subsequently the teaching profession, and the extent to which they engage with their courses and the teaching profession.' Dörnyei and Ushioda (2011) highlighted the two dimensions of teacher motivation in accordance with their conceptions of motivation; namely, the motivation to teach and the motivation to remain in the profession.

In their review article, Han, Yin and Boylan (2016) merge Sinclair's and Dörnyei and Ushioda's findings and state, 'Therefore, teacher motivation refers to reasons that [emanate] from individuals' intrinsic values to choose to teach and sustaining teaching, and the intensity of teacher motivation which is indicated by effort expended on teaching as influenced by a number of contextual factors.'

Of course, Berger recognises the part that pay plays in this contextualisation and calls for 'a salary structure that acknowledges the importance of the profession' but also says 'that improved salaries won't solve the problem'. This is a pertinent and age-old discussion in the UK and one that I am sure most teachers will have an opinion on. I tend to agree with Berger but as Sam Sims (2018) writes when he looked at whether increasing pay was more important than tackling workload, it's clear that it is not an either/or situation. Workload needs to be tackled but increasing pay as a 'retention policy would be better value for money than the current approach of trying to incentivise recruitment – which is akin to topping up a leaky bucket'.

For Berger, it all boils down to the fact that, 'A strong teacher won't stay in the profession very long unless she (they) is given the time, respect, resources and support necessary to be proud of her (their) work.' He goes on to deepen what is for me at the heart of teacher excellence: 'Teachers want a work schedule that honors their need for time for planning, preparation, reflection, research and collaboration ... They want professional respect and growth to be integral to their work. And they want some breathing room...'

One such solution is the idea of 'the research-sensitive school' as outlined in the Institute for Effective Education (IEE) report (2021). It describes the research-sensitive school that has created a culture and framework that allows teachers to focus on teaching and learning. Teachers are reflective practitioners, working alone and with others to develop their practice with innovation, research evidence and evaluation. The report discusses constraints such as autonomy (in a similar way to Berger) but writes that 'teachers must work within these constraints to identify their own area for development'. Again like Berger, the report is clear that teachers cannot do this alone.

Point 8 of the IEE executive summary states, 'Research-sensitive schools are isolated examples of practice. To be sustained and spread, they need a supportive infrastructure at local, regional and national level. This would include adequate funding, a supportive policy framework, a reciprocal relationship with the research community, and, of course, evaluation of the research-sensitive school approach to establish that it is more effective.' For me, this goes to the heart of Berger's third toolbox, Teaching of Excellence.

The scholarship of teaching

Berger details his work with such teacher scholars with a genuine admiration and awe for what they are wanting to achieve within their classrooms. Upon reading his stories, you cannot help but be inspired. He also talks about his own experiences at Harvard by taking it full circle ... back to school culture. 'The heart of my one scholarship and reflective practice has been my school itself. I'm blessed to be a member of staff that plans together, gives advice and critique, challenges each other and supports and respects each other.'

Teaching in the UK

For me, this is an absolutely fascinating final toolbox and one that places itself right at the forefront of current discussions about the centrality and interdependence of quality curriculum design and effective, evidence-informed professional development. For Berger, in the US at that time, there was too much of a focus on a 'teacher-proof curriculum', where the development of teacher excellence was being sidelined, or focused on only by the few. For Berger, this was far too short-sighted: 'I'm not sure what these people are thinking.'

In the UK, the Teachers' Standards (Department for Education, 2012: updated in 2021) set out the parameters for teacher excellence at the start of their careers. The preamble states, 'Teachers make the education of their pupils their first concern, and are accountable for achieving the highest possible standards in work and conduct. Teachers act with honesty and integrity; have strong subject knowledge, keep their knowledge and skills as teachers up-to-date and are self-critical; forge positive professional relationships; and work with parents in the best interests of their pupils.' It relied on individual schools, academies or MATs to ensure the standards were enacted, or even truly achievable within the context of such differing school provision; or even codifiable, in terms of the Standards as an immeasurable progression model (Fordham, 2017). Over time, the Standards became a part of school practice for NQT induction, but the questions began to surface such as:

- What happens when the NQT year is successfully completed?
- What does teacher career development and professional development look like for those teachers and all the other teachers, who have been teaching for three years or more?

The Sutton Trust report (2015) stated, 'Too many educators we entrust with the learning of our children do not themselves have high quality learning opportunities. In the battle to improve social mobility it seems an obvious priority area to act upon immediately: we know that within schools the quality of classroom teaching has by far the biggest impact on pupils, particularly those from poorer homes.' It seems no coincidence that following such a high-profile report, in July 2016 the Department for Education published Standard for Teachers' Professional Development. It was headlined with the now famous Dylan Wiliam quote, 'Every teacher needs to improve, not because they are not good enough, but because they can be even better.'

The Standard covered five areas:

- Professional development should have a focus on improving and evaluating pupil outcomes.
- Professional development should be underpinned by robust evidence and expertise.
- Professional development should include collaboration and expert challenge.
- Professional development programmes should be sustained over time.

And all this is underpinned by, and requires that:

- Professional development must be prioritised by school leadership. (DfE, 2016)

All of these are admirable but once again, concerns began to surface, as the teacher retention and recruitment figures began to soar, particularly in areas of high disadvantage that actually needed their teachers 'to get even better' in order for their children to succeed. For Berger, the answer lies in clear opportunities for scholarship within the profession.

For me, the UK's response to these concerns dictated the scholarship journey that has manifested itself over a number of years to today:

- Teacher Recruitment and Retention Strategy (DfE, 2019a), which outlines changes to teaching and leadership pathways.
- The Early Career Framework (DfE, 2019b) described as, 'The definitive move toward the importance of high quality, evidence-informed teaching and professional development – school led/leadership driven.'
- In 2021, a (fully funded) suite of new and revamped National Professional Qualifications (NPQs).

Despite some reservations about these qualifications from some quarters, I get the impression that Ron Berger would be pleased with these opportunities for teaching excellence.

The importance of scholarship at St Matthew's

We haven't always valued 'scholarship' as described by Berger but what we have consistently valued is being 'research sensitive'. It was because of this that we applied to become a Research School. Over time, as our own understanding of evidence-informed practice and the 'best bets' for improving outcomes for disadvantaged students have deepened; we have developed what we refer to as a teacher development pathway, which includes more 'scholarly' opportunities, that will hopefully impact directly back into the classroom.

The great Viviane Robinson (2007) writes, '... the more leaders focus their relationships, their work and their learning on the core business of teaching and learning, the greater their influence on student outcome.'

Our 'focus on the core business' means that across the staff team, we are doing/ will be doing the following training:

- Headteacher – Leverage Leadership Institute – Instructional Coaching.
- DHT – NPQH.
- AHT – Curriculum Leadership training.
- Lead Practitioner – Leverage Leadership.
- Previous AHT – Masters in Expert Teaching.
- Key Stage Leaders – new NPQs.

To deepen our teacher excellence, we are also using the following materials:

- The Great Teaching Toolkit (Coe et al., 2020).

- The EEF Guide to Supporting School Planning (EEF, 2020), which as it states, 'aims to support school leaders with their planning for the year 2021.' It focuses on:

  - High-quality teaching.
  - Targeted academic support.
  - Wider strategies.

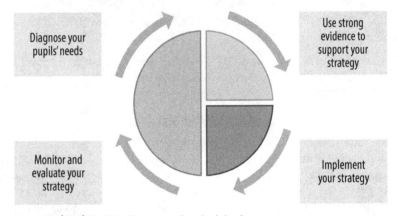

Source: EEF (2020) The EEF guide to supporting school planning.

- The EEF Effective Professional Development Guidance Report (EEF, 2021). The suite of materials provides a judicious guide to supporting the design and delivery of quality professional development. As it states: 'PD has great potential; but it also comes with costs. We know that teachers engage in professional development activities whilst balancing multiple and, at times, competing commitments and time pressures. The need is clear, therefore, for PD to be well-designed, selected, and implemented so that the investment is justified.'

EEF PD website

To end this chapter, I turn to Genders and Barber (2021), who sum up our school and I hope Berger's vision perfectly, when writing about the new NPQs.

'This is a call back to teacher excellence. Through pursuing excellence in teaching and working together for the common good, we will be enacting social justice for every community.'

Active ingredients: Teaching of Excellence is...

- An understanding that if schools are to improve, it must begin in the classroom, with teachers.

- An assumption that strong teachers view their profession as a calling. They want an environment that respects and supports the growth of their teaching practice. When teachers are excited and passionate, students get excited and passionate – find the beauty in your subject and embrace an ethic of excellence.

- A view that teaching is a craft – it takes time and support to get it right.

- An expectation that teachers should see themselves as scholars – reading, researching, observing others and identifying best practice.

References.

Coe, R., Rauch, C. J., Kime, S. and Singleton D. (2020) *Great teaching toolkit: Evidence review.* Available at: www.cambridgeinternational.org/Images/584543-great-teaching-toolkit-evidence-review.pdf (Accessed: 13 January 2022).

Department for Education. (2012. Updated 2021) *Teachers' Standards.* London: Crown.

Department for Education. (2016) *Standard for teachers' professional development.* London: Crown.

Department for Education. (2019a) *Teacher recruitment and retention strategy.* London: Crown.

Department for Education. (2019b) *Early career framework.* London: Crown.

Department for Education. (2020) *National professional qualifications frameworks.* London: Crown.

Dörnyei, Z. and Ushioda, E. (2011) *Teaching and researching motivation.* 2nd ed. New York, NY: Longman.

EEF. (2020) *The EEF guide to supporting school planning: A tiered approach to 2021.* Available at: https://educationendowmentfoundation.org.uk/public/files/Publications/Covid-19_Resources/The_EEF_guide_to_supporting_school_planning_-_A_tiered_approach_to_2021.pdf (Accessed: 13 January 2022).

EEF. (2021) *Effective professional development: Guidance report.* Available at: https:// d2tic4wvo1iusb.cloudfront.net/eef-guidance-reports/effective-professional-development/EEF-Effective-Professional-Development-Guidance-Report.pdf (Accessed: 21 January 2022).

Fordham, M. (2017) *Are the Teachers' Standards fit for purpose?* Blog. Available at: https:// clioetcetera.com/2017/12/17/are-the-teachers-standards-fit-for-purpose/ (Accessed: 21 December 2021).

Genders, N. and Barber, P. (2021) *Leading a culture of teacher excellence.* Catholic Education Service.

Institute for Effective Education. (2021) *The open door: How to be a research-sensitive school.* Available at: https://the-iee.org.uk/the-open-door/ (Accessed: 20 December 2021).

Han, J., Yin, H. and Boylan, M. (Reviewing Editor) (2016) 'Teacher motivation: Definition, research development and implications for teachers.' *Cogent Education,* 3(1).

Robinson, V. (2007) *The impact of leadership on student outcomes: Making sense of the evidence.* Available at: https://research.acer.edu.au/research_conference_2007/5 (Accessed: 22 December 2021).

Sims, S. (2018) *Is pay more important than workload for teacher retention?* Blog. Education Policy Institute. Available at: https://epi.org.uk/publications-and-research/teacher-retention-pay-workload/ (Accessed: 21 December 2021).

Sinclair, C. (2008) 'Initial and changing student teacher motivation and commitment to teaching.' *Asia-Pacific Journal of Teacher Education,* 36(2): pp. 79-104.

Sutton Trust. (2015) *Developing teachers: Improving professional development for teachers.* Available at: https://www.suttontrust.com/wp-content/uploads/2019/12/Developing-Teachers-1. pdf (Accessed: 21 December 2021).

CONCLUSION

A CALL TO EXCELLENCE

SONIA THOMPSON

'… a reminder: I have no blueprint to share: this isn't a quick fix. It's an ethic, an approach, a way of thinking … reflect on where in their culture they see quality. What do you think contributes to the success in these realms and what prevents it in other places?'

Ron Berger

Through his toolboxes, Berger has set out a pathway for teachers and schools to imprint excellence into their culture framework. I hope, through signposting you to the evidence that supports the approaches within the toolboxes and presenting our examples and case studies, this *In Action* book has at least given you some food for thought.

Of course, having read it, you may feel that it exemplifies your practice. Berger would urge you to identify what it is in your school context and what affords you this success? It is through this identification that practice not only becomes perfect, but it becomes permanent. Of course, there is also the argument that school improvement is never finished.

If you have read this and you feel a moral imperative to strive towards greatness, then for me, Berger would urge you to unpick this and begin to plan your pathway. In doing this, it would be remiss of me to not signpost readers to the EEF guidance document, Putting Evidence to Work: A School's Guide to Implementation (2021).

I agree with Bambrick-Santoyo (2021) when he writes that, 'Excellence is not an act but a habit.' Habits are formed when things are done persistently and consistently, and Berger acknowledges the many competing factors that can impede this journey to excellence. But may I take you back to Austin's Butterfly and what for me is the golden thread of *An Ethic of Excellence*:

'The progress of the drawing, from a primitive first draft to an impressive final is a powerful message for educators ... we often settle for low-quality work because we underestimate the capacity of students to create great work. With time, clarity, critique and support, students are capable of much more than we imagine.'

Surely, we all want this as an ethic of excellence for all of our students.

References.

Bambrick-Santoyo, P. and Chiger, S. (2021) *Love and literacy: A practical guide for grades 5-12 to finding the magic in literature.* NJ: Jossy-Bass.

EEF. (2021) *Putting evidence to work: A school's guide to implementation.* Available at: https://d2tic4wvo1iusb.cloudfront.net/eef-guidance-reports/implementation/EEF_Implementation_Guidance_Report_2019.pdf (Accessed: 22 December 2021).

APPENDIX

Case study

Name of lead teacher/s, department and school

Sarah Needham and Ange Daly – Curriculum leader and assistant curriculum leader for art and photography – Chorlton High School

Alice Girault – Assistant Headteacher – Chorlton High School

The ethic of excellence you exemplified. Why?

We exemplified the five principles as they underpin our approach to curriculum and assessment and showcase the ethic of excellence that we pursue in all of our students.

Your process for embedding the ethic of excellence into practice.

1. Assign work that matters.

- Our curriculum is forever evolving. We are fortunate within our subject to be able to respond quickly to current events (exploring the work of Shamsia Hassani, a street artist working in Kabul, commenting on the

recent troubles, for example). Recently we have made changes to ensure our selected artists reflect our drive for a conscientious curriculum ensuring women and LGBTQ+ artists are represented and of course we are continually striving to develop an anti-racist curriculum.

- Our curriculum is written as a team, however, individual staff shape lessons around the students they teach. Staff continually research, visit galleries and practice their specialism enriching their delivery.

- We ensure our work is relevant for those who love to create with a skills-based curriculum (exploration of formal elements) but ensure we support those who want to appreciate art but are not confident in doing so (art history/contextual studies/stories). No cheese plant drawing.

- Our curriculum and assessment are outcome based. Accessibility is ensured by artist/skill choice and giving the tools to enable students to make a *personal* response as required by the assessment objectives.

2. Study examples of excellence.

- Using the displays as examples of excellence is a really useful teaching tool. Students find it inspirational, aspirational and motivational.

- We use the displayed examples to unpick what makes them excellent.

- We identify the qualities of success in a displayed piece of work, and this becomes the students' success criteria for their own work.

- Often the displays can be removed from the walls and used as a scaffold for weaker students.

- Having displays in the classrooms allows students to become skilled in self-regulating the quality of their own work. They understand it's a standard for them to aim for.

- Staff update and change displays regularly to reflect the current curriculum or a critique planned for during class time.

3. Build a culture of critique.

- Celebration Station at the beginning, middle or end of a lesson – a pivot for group discussion reviewing and planning.

- The Chain Game acts as a group critique. The teacher picks a piece of work to highlight how a student has met the given criteria and models language to explain improvements. The chosen student's work will then copy the same process/language using another student's work as an example and so on.

4. Require multiple revisions.

- Don't accept the first piece of work.
- Initial work/idea is rarely the best.
- Develop work by discussion, feedback, thumbnail studies, try outs and mock-ups.
- Look at exam board requirements or one of the assessment objectives.
- What is acceptable for the student is often shaped and changed by the culture of excellence in the department. Our talented students, rather than deplete confidence of other students, actually raise the bar and improve overall quality because of the way staff use peer work as a teaching tool.

5. Provide opportunities for public presentation.

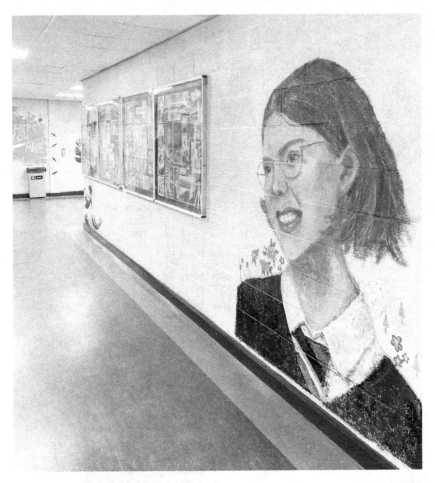

- 'Ethic of Excellence Gallery' in the corridors.
- End of year exhibition – all art students present at least one piece of artwork.
- Displays on walls in classrooms.
- Modelling within lessons using PowerPoints (photos of students' work).
- 'Glory Tour' – students can show their work to another class/teacher.
- Celebration Station – pupils leave work on display for other classes to see.
- The socials – work is shared on Instagram; more so at KS3 as the exam boards are resistant to sharing live coursework.

What have you achieved/hope to achieve in the future?

- We have created and shaped what we believe is an inspiring environment that engages and excites all our students and staff alike.

- The uptake of our subjects remains consistently high and our results for our students are some of the highest in the school.

- The art department has become a special place for many of our students who find sanctuary in the inclusive environment.

- It is our intention to continually update our displays in and out of the classroom to respond to the everchanging world that our students experience. Most of all, we want every student to see themselves reflected within the work and to be active participants in its creation.

CPSIA information can be obtained
at www.ICGtesting.com
Printed in the USA
JSHW020508070322
23556JS00004B/6